Night Songs

LIFE IN THE MIDST OF DEATH

Phyllis L. Mayo

Night Songs

© 2021 Phyllis L. Mayo

Paperback ISBN: 978-1-66780-349-4
eBook ISBN: 978-1–66780-350-0

To my dear friend Marshall
who opened doors of opportunity to me
that I might experience the life
I have lived within the walls of Springmoor.

- and -

To the memory of beloved Hannah
who first and fervently
encouraged me to
"Write it down!"

- and -

To the Great Cloud of Witnesses
who surround me
and profoundly touch
the spirit in me.
(Hebrews 12: 1)

CONTENTS

HOW CAN I KEEP FROM SINGING?

My life flows on in endless song, above earth's lamentation.

I hear the real though far off hymn that hails a new creation.

Through all the tumult and the strife, I hear the music ringing.

It sounds an echo in my soul.

How can I keep from singing?

What though my joys and comforts die, the Lord my Savior liveth.

What though the darkness gather round,

songs in the night he giveth.

No storm can shake my inmost calm while to that refuge clinging.

Since Christ is Lord of heav'n and earth,

how can I keep from singing?

I lift mine eyes; the cloud grows thin; I see the blue above it.

And day by day this pathway smooths,

since first I learned to love it.

The peace of Christ makes fresh my heart,

a fountain ever springing.

All things are mine since I am his.

How can I keep from singing?

HOW CAN I KEEP FROM SINGING?
Words written by Robert Lowry, 1860
(Public Domain)

INTRODUCTION

On August 6, 1984, I began work at Springmoor, a spanking brand-new continuing care retirement community in Raleigh, North Carolina. Most of my first year was spent doing odd jobs since the first group of residents moved in gradually over the span of a year or more. The next spring when the health care center opened, I became activities director, which involved a lot of going from room to room rounding up people for Bingo or Bible study. When the State of North Carolina required the facility to have a social worker, I was assigned the job even though I had no experience. So, while I worked full time, including evenings, I went to school part time over a period of three years at the University of North Carolina at Chapel Hill to earn a master's degree in social work. Because I already had a master of divinity degree, eventually I was entrusted with the privilege of becoming the founding chaplain for Springmoor.

Growing up from first grade in Stantonsburg, a small Wilson County town in Eastern North Carolina, I lived across the street from the Baptist church and attended almost every time the doors were open. Since the only other denominations in town were the Methodist and Pentecostal Holiness churches, my exposure to various denominations was limited to say the least.

In my developmental years as chaplain—and it was a steep learning curve—I came to appreciate much about other Christian denominations. One book I have found to be particularly rich in content and meaning is *The Book of Common Prayer*. There are bits and pieces of prayers that lift my spirit to the heights of hope and joy. As I read the powerful and sacred words, I recall the anointing of sick and dying people I have known and loved. I recall memorial services and burials. I cherish much of this traditional expression of faith. Yet there is one line, the first line of The Committal Service of Burial Rite I, that always catches me up short.

Every time I hear or read the ancient words, "In the midst of life we are in death," I think, "That sounds backward to me. There is more, much more to this story." In fact, I believe that line should, at the least, be amended to read, "In the midst of life we are in death, *yet in death we are in the midst of life.*" That is what my experience tells me anyway.

Over a period of thirty-five years, seven as social worker and then twenty-eight as chaplain, I sat with literally hundreds of people as they died, or joined families at bedsides just after the death of a loved one. Death is, indeed, in the midst of our lives, as individuals and in community. Yet in those moments when last breaths have been taken and everyone stands in awe of what we have witnessed, even in the midst of death, there is most definitely life.

Now, more than a year into my retirement, I find that the stories are coming to me as songs in the night. I go to bed. I lie there. Faces and long-past events move from my heart to my head as songs of life and death and life. And so, I share the stories of the life I have seen and experienced, even in the midst of death. My stories began in childhood and will no doubt continue until my time to die comes. What a privilege. What glorious and holy times they have been.

LIFE AND DEATH AND LIFE

Not long ago I was talking with a friend about someone dear to us who had died, and in the conversation, I said, "Well, she's with her husband." My friend, who is now ninety years old and a committed and thoughtful Christian, replied, "Do you really think so?" Then he went on to tell me that in the opinion of his highly regarded theologian friend, there is no indication in the Bible that such a belief is true. I have been contemplating that question since the conversation with my friend, as I have been since my father died when my mother was forty-nine years old and asking the same question.

I believe 100 percent that when we die, *we shall be with God.* Everything beyond that is up for grabs. The where, the how, the what. But I do think there are some Biblical passages that hint at a knowledge of others in heaven.

First, I think trying to explain whether or how a married couple will still be married in heaven is impossible. For example, think about holidays. If someone has been happily married, then is widowed, and then has another happy marriage, who will determine in whose presence the endless heavenly celebrations will happen? The best answer I can venture to offer to that hypothetical question is "at God's banquet table where all the children of God will be gathered as one body" with God as the central figure of celebration and love.

Second and third are questions of how old we will be and what our bodies will be like if we are to know each other in heaven. If a child dies, will that person still be a child in heaven? Or will we all be the same age? Will all our bodies be perfect in form and function and free from earthly impediments? I believe the only answer to these questions comes from I John 3: 2. ". . . what we will be has not yet been made known . . . we shall be like him, for we shall see him as he is." (NIV) I find that very satisfying.

The fourth confirmation of some sort of "known" existence in heaven comes from Hebrews, chapters 11 and 12. When the writer refers to the "great cloud of witnesses" who surround us, I can almost see them and sometimes feel them near. I believe that when we die, we become some sort of new and perfected creation, someone who is living, witnessing, watching, and worshiping.

This may be simplistic thinking, but it is what I believe. I believe that what we shall yet be and see is beyond our comprehension, for being with God face to face is more than we can fathom in our current limited understanding and imagination. You will find these beliefs reflected in the "songs" of this book. No doubt you have your own stories by day or songs in the night as well.

SONG 1 -

THE COLORING BOOK

We were friends, Eleanor and I. Playmates still too young for school. We lived down the street from each other in the small, idyllic town in Eastern North Carolina where children were free to roam up and down the sidewalks and go in and out of each other's homes, left to play for hours on end, being closely watched all the while by our mothers who were busy ironing, cleaning, cooking, canning, and otherwise making nice homes for us.

Though we must have cut out paper dolls, jumped rope, and played "house," I do not remember those things. I just remember that Eleanor got sick.

Eleanor's sickness was more than just a sore throat or the measles or a hurt leg. She was sick for a long time. She could not play with me. I missed my friend.

My gentle and caring mother helped me. Though I do not actually remember doing it, I feel sure we shopped together for a coloring book for Eleanor. But I do remember what happened next.

Mama and I walked down the street to Eleanor's house. While Mama stood a respectful distance behind me on the sidewalk leading up to the house, I was the one who climbed the steps and came into the deep shade of the front porch to knock on the screen door behind which the wooden door stood open.

"I brought this coloring book for Eleanor."

"Oh, thank you so much," said the smiling, kind, adult female, most likely Eleanor's mother, who had come to the door. "I'll give it to her. I know she'll like it. But she doesn't feel like playing today."

That was my last visit to Eleanor's house. She died a short time later. But in my heart, I have stood many, many times on that porch bearing a coloring book, with my wise mother at my back, tenderly introducing me to death.

SONG 2 –

THE PILLOW

My grandmother was in her early eighties. She was small and wiry and had not been well for a long while. I never knew her as a snuggly, playful, loving grandmother. In reality, I was somewhat uncomfortable around her, frightened by her physical frailty I did not understand, and the need to be quiet when she was visiting with us for a month or two.

And then she died.

My father's brother and his family lived in Baltimore. They had come "down home to Carolina" for a couple of days to visit Grandmama, knowing that her time to live was short. When they left, they took my seven-years-older-than-me sister, Barbara, with them for a few days at the beach, leaving me and my younger sister, Teresa, at home with our parents. Grandmama's death came sooner than expected, and so they returned to stay with us for the time leading up to the funeral.

When they arrived, I saw my father cry for the first time. As brother greeted brother, and sisters-in-law hugged, the cousins were left in the wake of adult grief. A time now, unquestionably, to be hushed and respectful.

Our house was well-suited for our family but not large enough to comfortably accommodate another whole family. So, as we were accustomed to doing when visitors came, the children bedded down on sleeping pallets made of quilts and blankets placed on the floor, while the adults were given the children's beds.

It was a comfort to have my older sister back home to offer some stability to me in the midst of the disorder that inevitably comes with death. I was six years old, and her maturity and presence mattered.

As we settled down for the night, I was glad to be sleeping with Barbara. I crawled into the makeshift bed first. Then, when Barbara came to bed, we became aware there were not enough pillows. There was only one on our pallet. Not wanting to give up my pillow, but not wanting her to be without one, I slipped the pillow over toward Barbara and said, "Here, we can share."

Pallets on the floor and shared pillows will always remind me of my grandmother's final rest, and of the comfort of having my sister at my side.

SONG 3 –

THREE WORDS OF PARTING

Max and Barbara moved with their two children, Suzanne, four years old, and Joel, two years old, to my hometown when I was eleven years old. They came from the Upstate region of South Carolina to Stantonsburg in Eastern North Carolina where Max had accepted the call to be pastor of the Baptist church. We loved them from the very beginning.

Not only was Max the pastor, preaching, visiting the sick, and all other pastoral duties, he was also the church secretary and the choir director. Barbara was the church organist. The church certainly got our money's worth and much, much more. I fear Max and Barbara got the short end of the stick, at least in the early years of their ministry.

Suzanne and Joel were beautiful children. Suzanne had dark wavy hair and Joel was blond. I was a frequent babysitter for them, even spending the night when their parents were out of town for meetings.

When they first arrived, Max, who was no more than five feet and six or seven inches tall, was slim, a normal weight for his height. But after a couple of years passed, he began putting on a lot of extra weight. The home cooking of the women and a few of the men of the church was just too tempting. And my mama's biscuits were a huge culprit.

Each day in the late afternoon, Max worked in his office at the church which was directly across the street beside our house. Although the exit from the church nearest his office was the more direct way for him to walk home, he began making a habit of coming out of another door in the direction of our house, straight toward our kitchen door, just as Mama was making the biscuits. Since his wife, Barbara, was at home teaching piano lessons, and her dinner would not be ready for another hour or two, Max often ate with us. He loved watching Mama make the biscuits and teased her about "knuckling" each one as she placed it on the tray before baking. She simply, it seemed, could not place those biscuits without a little press from her knuckle. That made them all the better.

Eventually, Max decided he needed to lose all the extra weight and went on a strict diet. The weight seemed to pour off him. A friend of mine who was casually acquainted with Max and Barbara saw them in the grocery story one day. She had not yet seen him without the extra weight, and when she saw them that day, Max newly slim, she thought for a little while that Barbara was with another man. No. No. No.

As with many small towns, there were only a few churches in and around Stantonsburg. The Methodist church was on the far end of the block from the Baptist church, and the Pentecostal Holiness church was on the edge of town. So if the white people in town were members of any church, they were likely members of one of those three churches. This means, among many other things, that Max not only preached hundreds of sermons, but also officiated hundreds of weddings, funerals, and baptisms. He did all those things for my family.

My father was not a member of the church for most of his life. He had no objections to church and did not discount its value, but since he had to be up quite early during the week for work and usually on Saturdays for working in the garden or the yard, Sundays offered good opportunities to sleep a little later. When one of my sisters or I had a special role in a service, he was usually there. My mother saw to it that we were at church for Sunday school and worship services on Sundays as well as age-appropriate organizations and choir practice during the week.

As Max learned to love my mother's biscuits, he and my father developed a close friendship. And then Max led my father to accept Christ as his Savior.

Daddy joined the church, started studying the Bible, attended Sunday school and worship, joined the choir, and eventually became a deacon. The church and the church family became an important part of his life. Our family's life of faith was complete. Max and Daddy became exceptionally good friends, and our families sometimes enjoyed social events together, like grilling chicken or making homemade ice cream. Then after about five years, my father died suddenly. This was quite hard for Max. He was a great help to Mama, my sisters, and me, not only with the funeral but in the aftermath as well.

Max and Barbara were supportive of me as I moved through my college years majoring in music. Since they were both musicians, this strengthened our bond. I do have to admit, however, that sometimes I would get aggravated with him when he would, at the last minute on Sunday evening, say, "Phyllis, you're singing tonight." I would hiss and growl and carry on, then my gentle, reasonable mother would calm me down, and I would agree to sing.

Time passed. Years passed. Max was pastor for twenty-five years. Then thirty-five. And ultimately forty-five. All this time he continued to direct the choir, and Barbara continued playing the organ.

During the last ten years or so of his life, Max had three different cancers. Each time, he had grueling treatments, but he continued to preach. In fact, there were few Sundays he missed. Toward the end of his life, all the church members, who cared for and loved him, were much concerned because of his physical weakness, but his spiritual strength was greater. He preached just a couple of Sundays before he died.

On the weekend that Max was dying, my sister called to let me know he would not live much longer. I had to see him. When I arrived, Max and Barbara's extended family had gathered and were joined by a steady stream of church members coming and going, old and young. I knew Max was weak and could not tolerate a long visit, nor did I want to have a long visit. I needed to say three things.

Barbara graciously invited me into the bedroom. Max was not fully alert but was awake enough to hear and understand what was being said and to respond, perhaps, with a word or two. I drew close to his ear, saying what I had come to say. "I love you. Thank you for being my friend. And thank you for leading my daddy to know the Lord."

He smiled and nodded. Tears welled up in our eyes as I gave him a kiss on the cheek.

A night or two later, Barbara crawled into bed with Max as usual. When she awoke during the night, she found that he had peacefully died.

I was privileged to lead his funeral service. It was in the evening on the same day I sang in the afternoon for the service of my dear friend and accompanist Carol. Heaven's music that day was more beautiful than ever.

> *"How beautiful are the feet of them that preach the*
> *gospel of peace and bring glad tidings of good things!"*
>
> *(Romans 10: 15 KJV)*

SONG 4 –

A

She arrived in a 1960s-era green Volkswagen Beetle. Her name was Mrs. Cobb. She was one of the best gifts that ever happened to me.

The small town in which I grew up had an elementary school, grades one through eight. A piano teacher who lived in town came periodically to give us music classes. Several grades would gather in the large Auditorium, and she would lead us in singing some songs. This teacher died suddenly one day at home, leaving us with no one other than our classroom teachers to offer any sort of music instruction. Some were capable, others were not. Then, as though out of my dreams, Mrs. Cobb appeared.

I was in fifth grade. Mrs. Cobb, the mother of four children, one of whom was less than a year old, lived in a neighboring county and had taken the job as music teacher for *all* the schools in our county. I loved her from the first day she came.

The students' time with her was usually spent in our regular classroom where we sat in our desks, all in rows. Mrs. Cobb would stand at the front of the class to teach new songs then she would walk up and down the aisles between the desks as we sang. One day when she came alongside my desk, she bent over and leaned in toward me to listen. "She thinks I can sing!" My heart flipped over with joy and excitement.

As that fall semester continued, I began to have an idea of what her schedule might be for coming to our school. I knew where she parked, and every day when I got a chance, coming in from recess, going to lunch, looking out the window, I watched that spot to see if her car was there. Each time she came was a happy time for me. Then one day I got up nerve to ask her if she would teach me voice lessons. I had no concept of the extremely busy life she lived, nor did she convey that to me. She just smiled warmly, with a glimmer in her dark brown eyes, and said "no" she could not do that, but she *would* help me as much as possible any time she came. That was good enough for me.

The years passed and Mrs. Cobb stayed with us in Wilson County Schools. When we finished grammar school and went to high school, life got even better. There we could sign up for choir as a class. It was an exciting opportunity for all the students who loved music. I sang in the large choir and in the smaller vocal ensemble. I made some wonderful friends in those two groups, and Mrs. Cobb became "ours." When she occasionally talked about one of her other schools, we were a bit jealous, but we also realized that she had to go to them as well. So we just had to live with it! (In fact, they loved her too, and I feel sure she made them feel as special as she made us feel.)

One of the people in the choir and vocal ensemble was Chet, who lived three houses down the street from me. He was a Mrs. Cobb groupie as well. In summers after we had learned to drive, we would go, on occasion, to her house. Though we were supposed to be helping her with some work, we just wanted to see her. We would always end up at her piano playing and singing.

One of the most wonderful aspects of Mrs. Cobb's life was her family. She had an incredibly supportive husband. He was a bank president in their small town, yet he made time to attend all the concerts her students presented, bringing with him the four children. So as time passed, I and others got to know the whole family. They were not only kind and well-mannered but also a devoted and loving family. John Vines Cobb was a lay leader in their church, was at one time mayor of their town, and was a county commissioner. Mrs. Cobb directed the church choir, and almost the entire family sang in that choir. Each of the children got to know me and welcomed me to their home and into their lives. I even had an opportunity to meet the grandmothers, Mama Cobb and Nettie Pitts. Nettie, Mrs. Cobb's mother, gave me the highest compliment when she said my singing reminded her of Mrs. Cobb when she was a young girl.

When I was in tenth grade, Mrs. Cobb presented to me the idea of auditioning for the North Carolina Governor's School. One young man, a year ahead of me in school, had attended the previous summer with a specialization in piano performance. She wanted me to audition for the vocal performance program. I auditioned and was accepted. By the time I graduated from high school two years later, eight more people from our school were accepted into that same summer program. Mrs. Cobb was not only a teacher but a true mentor and friend, opening doors of which we had never dreamed.

I majored in music in college with thoughts of being the kind of teacher Mrs. Cobb was. I was not fortunate to have her for my practice teaching experience, and the blessedly short teaching situation in which I did find myself put an end to any notions I might have had of becoming a teacher. I was simply not cut from that special cloth. But I did continue to sing and even went to graduate school in vocal performance. Mrs. Cobb was *always* there for me in spirit, in support, and in person when she could be.

As I entered the working world, we kept in touch. My younger sister, Teresa, married Ralph who was a close friend of the Cobbs, and I often received news of the Cobb clan through him since the two families lived just a few miles apart.

There came a time when calling my mentor and friend Mrs. Cobb became awkward. I was older, and she wanted me to call her Ann, but I struggled with that and never really found it comfortable. Then when she had grandchildren, they called her "A." It was perfect for me as well.

I am not sure why the grandchildren called her A, but I know why it was a fit for me. Every summer when she spent a couple of weeks at the beach with her family, she would send a postcard to me. She made her handwriting as small as possible, filling up the entire card, writing all around the edges, and ending all sentences with exclamation marks. Then down in a tiny corner, teetering on the edge of the card, she would sign, "Love A." She never left enough room or had enough time, it seemed, to write Ann. That was A!!!! (All exclamations marks in memory of her!)

Many years of friendship passed. She sang for my father's funeral. I rejoiced with her when her children graduated, married, and had their own children, or achieved other lofty goals. I sang for her and Vines' fiftieth wedding anniversary celebration. My teacher had, indeed, become and remained a dear, dear friend.

One evening I was ironing when I heard an exceptionally talented young girl singing on television. My very first thought was to call A. I did. She immediately tuned to that station and was as excited as I was to hear the young, fresh voice. We did not talk long for fear that we would miss the music. That was the last time I would talk with her.

Ralph called one evening a few months later and said, "Phyllis, I have some bad news. Mrs. Cobb is in the hospital and is in critical condition." She had become ill practically overnight and had surgery. The surgery did not go well, and she was not going to live. I thought long and hard about driving the hour and a half to the hospital but decided against it in consideration of the family and their need to spend their last treasured hours with her. They sang, I heard, around her bed all through her last days. Another friend, Page, who had been in the high school choir and had maintained a close relationship with A, called in a few days to tell me she had died. The world lost a brilliant light and beautiful voice that day.

I called the family the next day. They had been discussing the funeral and wanted to know if I would sing. My heart pounded just as it had when I first knew Mrs. Cobb was listening. Of course, I would sing. It would be the honor of my life.

The children, Vines, and I talked. I suggested a song I believed would be ideal for remembering the life of this wife, mother, music teacher, friend, and devoted Christian. They were not familiar with the song, but when I told them the title and read the words over the phone, we all knew it was perfect. The title: "How Can I Keep from Singing?" Teresa, Ralph, Chet, and Coley, another high school friend, and I joined their church choir for the funeral in the small Presbyterian church which overflowed with loving friends into the Sunday school rooms and the churchyard. The choir sang one of A's favorite anthems, "God So Loved the World." Page played piano and another dear friend, Alma, played the organ. A beloved former minister led the service, and Ann's son-in-law, a Presbyterian minister, spoke for the family. At the end of the service, as the family was beginning to depart, we sang with them the traditional Irish blessing, "May the Road Rise to Meet You."

Mrs. Cobb. Ann. A. One of the best gifts that ever happened to me.

And until we meet again, may God hold you, A, and all the world in the palm of His hand.

Amen and amen.

SONG 5 –

THE VISITING ANGEL

The boy lived down the street from me. He was in my class at school. He attended the same church I attended, only half a block away from his house.

Neither of the two ladies he lived with was the right age to be his mother. They had bluish hair and seemed more like maiden aunts. Where the parents were or what may have happened to them, I never knew.

When the children from all over town played together, he played with us too. We were a small-town, wholesome gang of kids, nine, ten, eleven years old. Loving life.

Then one summer day, we heard he had died, and even sadder, had been killed in an accident.

The story came like this: the boy had been riding in the open back of a pick-up truck and just seemed, almost, to have dived off. Of course, things get exaggerated, especially where a child and death *and an angel* are involved.

Over the next few days, word went around quickly among adults and children that the aunts were telling a story the boy had told them. On the morning of his death, he had related to them at breakfast that an angel had come and stood at the end of his bed during the night.

No sage or mystic was among us in our small town to interpret what all this meant. Surely the Baptist minister himself must have struggled to explain an angelic visitation and the death of an innocent child even as he invoked God's love and care in the midst of untimely death and grief.

There were a lot of questions and few answers. Had the boy been depressed and intentionally thrown himself out of the truck? Was it simply, and more likely, an accident when the truck slowed or accelerated too quickly or made an unexpected move? Was the death of this young boy predetermined by God and foretold by the angel?

As with all such tragedies, there have never been answers, not sufficient ones anyway.

This sad and unusual turn of events in my childhood did not make me dread going to sleep for fear that I too would be visited by an angel. With the passing of years, however, it sounds more and more like a comfort.

As the boy's body fell from the truck, I trust that very same visiting angel, already familiar to the boy in its glorious splendor, lifted him up and carried him away to a safe and loving new home.

SONG 6 –

THE BROTHERS BROTHERS

Aurora in Beaufort County, North Carolina, in the 1970s was rich black farmland, teeming waters, and salt of the earth people. If the men, and some of the women, were not farming or fishing, they were hunting.

And so it was in November 1971 that my father had gone "down home" to spend several days with his sister and her husband to hunt deer with the men in the family. Aunt Edna and Uncle Harvey Brothers had large farms which were tended at this point mostly by two of their sons, Harvey Jr. and Hubert. Soybeans and other crops provided a smorgasbord for literally hundreds and hundreds of deer. A hunter's paradise. I shall never forget going to those same fields to see the deer late one summer evening several years earlier. We witnessed a most unusual and magnificent sight for North Carolina: an aurora borealis. Shimmering green light spanning the northern sky appeared as a curtain of dancing waters.

It was late in the evening that November in 1971 when my father called home after a day of hunting. From the sound of my mother's voice, we knew something was terribly wrong. Hanging up the phone, she told us that David, our eleven-year-old cousin, grandson of Aunt Edna and Uncle Harvey, had been killed in an accident.

David had ridden on a tractor in his granddad's lap since he was old enough to sit up. All the boys had done this, and so it was a natural thing for him as well. And as soon as they were old enough to shift gears and reach the pedals, they were driving tractors on their own.

At dusk on this mid-November day, dinner was ready. David's mother, Thora, went outside and waved for him to put up the tractor and come in to eat. As he aimed onto the drive toward the barn, he cut short and turned the tractor over in a ditch. He was crushed underneath and died in the ambulance on the way to the hospital. Thora was not permitted to even see her youngest child.

David, a little pudgy, with impish face freckled like his mother, was a fun boy. He especially loved his granddad. One of the favorite stories about the two of them involved a ladder and a hammer. Uncle Harvey was on the ladder, and David, a little fellow at the time, was standing below the ladder "helping." Uncle Harvey dropped the hammer, striking a glancing blow to David's head. Unharmed, David scolded, "Granddaddy, you ought to watch your damn hammer!"

In the wake of his death, all our family gathered over the next days. Aunts and uncles and cousins came from near and as far away as Maryland and Florida. Mary, elegant with her blond hair and black mourning clothes, and handsome cousin Gilbert. Martha, an older cousin, putting her arm around me in love and reassurance. The kitchen running over with funeral food. The two surviving brothers moving aimlessly in the house, surrounded by people who wanted to pity and comfort them. Uncle Harvey Jr. and Aunt Millie and their two sons who lived an acre and a driveway down the road. David's Uncle Tommy and his family, and numerous other uncles, aunts, and young cousins. Thora isolated in the bedroom. Voices hushed. The grief thick. The thought of David being dead . . . unthinkable. His granddaddy exclaiming, questioning, "I've lived my life. Why couldn't it have been me?"

An accident. No answers.

I have been a singer since childhood and was asked to sing at the funeral. I was eighteen at the time. What I sang I do not remember, but I do remember how extremely sad and stunned we all were. Following the church service, we moved across the churchyard to the cemetery where our forebears had long since been buried. Now a fresh grave was there for a young boy.

The following April, David's two brothers, Gary and Ronnie, were in a car accident. The phone call gave the barest of details, but the facts were clear. Gary had died instantly. Miraculously, Ronnie had survived almost unscathed, physically. How could this be? How could this *possibly* be? Two accidents. Two healthy brothers now dead.

Again, the family gathered. Again, I sang for the funeral. Again, the mother, paralyzed with grief, could not attend the funeral. She never attended another family funeral. Not even the funeral of her third son, Ronnie, who died in another farm accident ten years later.

Ronnie Brothers was twenty-five when he died. He shared a serious relationship with his girlfriend, and there had been talk of marriage. It was not to be.

No sons, no marriages meant no grandchildren. Yet later on a visit my sisters and I made to Thora and Hubert, we learned Thora had started a business. She was making and dressing porcelain dolls. The name of her business: Granny's Dolls. She was, it seemed, making her grandchildren.

Life continued. But there were more deaths; these more expected and "appropriate" to age. Uncle Harvey died. Aunt Edna died. Daddy and Mama died. Other family members died. Hubert was always at the funerals, gathering with others at the cemetery where his three boys were buried side by side in a row with identical headstones. Always smiling his million-dollar smile. Always broken-hearted but never wearing it on his sleeve. Thora found her solace, her way to survive, at home.

My two sisters, Barbara and Teresa, and I visited Hubert and Thora many years later. By then my sisters were married with grown children and a few grandchildren. I was entrenched in my career. Still, I had never stopped thinking about the boys, the three brothers. They had been just a few years younger than I, and their deaths had affected me greatly.

As we visited, it became apparent that Thora's memory was failing. She told my sister, "I don't always know who he is," indicating Hubert. And Hubert shared the same sad fact with my other sister and me. But they were making it, surviving in their long-established-not-so-normal, normal lives, holding each other up and together.

We had a good visit that day. Their house had been updated but still the family room was without family, and it looked out over the place where two of the boys had died.

As we were leaving, I could not bring myself to say good-bye without saying something about the boys. I tried to keep it simple with words something such as, "I think about your boys often and will never forget them."

Hubert flashed his beautiful smile. But Thora was the one who spoke, she with her cute, wrinkled up, freckled nose, her sweet smile. "I may not remember everything anymore. But I know one thing. I know that when I die and I get to heaven, my boys are going to be standing there waiting for me."

Hubert and Thora died within a year and a half of each other, having grown to old age, having lived almost fifty years without their boys. They endured in love until the end. Then what a joyful heavenly reunion there surely was for the three Brothers brothers and the farmer and the dollmaker.

SONG 7 –

THE KISS

I was singing for two weddings the third Saturday in June 1972. One of the weddings was at my home church directly across the street beside our family's house. The other one was at a church about ten miles away. Both rehearsals were on Friday evening. The first, the one farther away, was at 6:00, and the second one, across the street, was at 7:30. Just enough time apart to make both if I hurried along.

Our house was situated on a corner lot with a large yard. In the backyard, my father had a beautiful and bountiful vegetable garden. When I was a child, a "Daddy's girl," I loved "helping" him. I fondly remember pulling radishes from the earth, wiping off the soil, and biting into the crunchy, bitter root. We pulled up bunches of small carrots and dug red potatoes. When I got a little older and could actually be of help, the fun became work, and I tended to manage finding other things to do instead. But I can still see Daddy out in the garden, tilling the soil, and then working alongside Mama, picking beans, cutting okra, and plucking big ripe juicy tomatoes from the caged-up vines.

That Friday afternoon in June, I mowed the grass in our yard. After I finished and went inside to bathe and get dressed, Daddy came home from work and noticed that I had missed a spot of grass about the size of our kitchen, so he mowed it. When I was dressed and ready to go, I realized something was not quite right with Daddy. He was not feeling well. But instead of worrying about him, I decided for some silly reason to be angry with him. (This was a coping-with-fear strategy, I have learned as I have matured in life, albeit a poor one.) I left home and went on my way to the first wedding rehearsal, not really mad, just out of the house.

When I returned home an hour and a half or so later, our yard was full of cars. This was not unusual, since church members often felt free to use our yard for parking if all the street parking was taken. With just a few minutes to spare, I parked, hopped out of the car, and was going to run into the house for a minute. My sister Barbara, her husband, and their two daughters, four and two years old, had arrived from out of town for the weekend. Barbara was seven and a half months pregnant with their third child. We all adored those little girls, Daddy especially, and were looking forward to another.

Driving into the yard, I did not yet know that the two weddings would go on without me. As I went toward the house, I was happy to see Barbara coming toward me. But before she could get to me, her four-year-old, Susan, ran ahead and said, "Granddaddy's gone to heaven." Not "Hey, Aunt Phyllis." But "Granddaddy's gone to heaven." *What is she saying?* The look on Barbara's face confirmed the truth of those words.

Daddy had been experiencing the beginnings of a heart attack when I decided to be mad with him. His condition grew worse in a very short time, and Mama drove him ten miles to the clinic where our beloved doctor practiced. Daddy walked in. Our doctor was out of town, but Daddy was quickly attended by another physician. Mama was instructed to go across the street to the hospital to get the admission process started. Daddy never made it to the hospital.

Between the time I left for the wedding rehearsal and when I arrived back home, the world had turned upside down. My fifty-three-year-old father, my daddy, was dead. Barbara was twenty-five. I was eighteen. Teresa was fifteen. Mama was, at forty-nine, a widow.

Almost immediately, phone calls were made to all the relatives on both sides of the family. On Saturday morning, our pastor, Max, went with Mama, Barbara, Teresa, and me to the funeral home to arrange for the service. It was to be held at our church on Sunday afternoon, less than forty-eight hours since Daddy had mowed the grass and had a fatal heart attack. The funeral would be on Father's Day.

When Sunday arrived, Daddy's extensive and loving family came, some arriving on short notice from out of state, and some coming from "down home." Aunt Edna and Uncle Harvey and their family were still deeply grieving the deaths of two grandsons only months earlier. Mama's sisters and brother, in-laws, and our cousins came as well.

As was customary, Daddy's body was brought to the church for an open casket viewing before the service. About an hour before people began to arrive, our entire family walked across the street for our own last viewing and our good-byes. Each person, in turn as they wished, stepped up to see his body, to touch him, to whisper a word, or to wipe a tear. When it was my turn, I touched him. This was my first experience of touching a dead body. And to touch the body of someone I adored was a heartrending experience. I remember that he felt hard and cold, not cuddly and warm as I had known and loved him. I don't remember crying, though I probably did. I remember something else. I kissed Daddy on the cheek.

The kiss was life-sustaining and formative for me. In that moment I realized, even said in my own mind and heart, "That's not my daddy. It's the body he lived in, but I know where he is." I knew in that instant that the body I was touching, the face I kissed, I would miss for the rest of my life. But I knew, knew as real as anything I had ever known, that my daddy's laughing, loving spirit was with God.

SONG 8 –

THE MOTHER

The white house across the street and two down from ours was typical for its time and place. A rocking chair porch spanned the front of the house, and big windows allowed light and cool breezes to flood in. Old Mrs. Powell, as my mother referred to her, and her middle-aged daughter, Peaches Powell, lived there. I loved that name . . . Peaches Powell. On my list of quirky names, it ranked high, together with my father's aunt's name, Plum Godley, and our neighbor, Mr. Jim Bill Applewhite. Today they could have been the names of pop musicians or actors like Pink or Billy Bob Thornton.

Somewhere along the way, someone figured out that a little rental income could be made by converting the small upstairs of the house into an apartment. To give privacy to all parties, a metal staircase was attached to the side of the house to access the apartment. The first people I recall living there were a couple, Dave and Jenny.

They moved in when I was just finishing high school and starting college. Since I lived at home for college, and they were just beginning their careers and were not too much older than I, we became friends. They joined our church, which was just across the street, and also the choir, where Jenny and I sometimes sat side by side.

When Dave had to work late or go out of town, Jenny and I went to movies. The one I remember most was strange to say the least: *Behold a Pale Horse* starring Anthony Quinn. When Dave was out of town on at least one occasion, I spent the night so Jenny would not have to stay alone.

It was not long before they had a big announcement. They were going to be parents. The baby boy born to them was adorable.

On a Friday afternoon in November 1972, Jenny left the school where she was a teacher then remembered she had forgotten to pick up her paycheck from the office. She returned, parked in front of the school, ran in and picked up the check, and went back to the car. She backed her VW Beetle onto the road in the path of a large truck. Most likely, she never knew what hit her.

I remember little about the funeral. I just remember that all the people who knew this sweet, loving couple with a small, precious child were devastated. We wanted to be helpful, but words, food, and flowers, even prayers, seemed far, far from adequate, could not fill the gaping hole in Dave's life.

After a few months, Dave moved out of town, away from the tiny apartment now cavernous without his beloved wife.

I do not know how the story ended for Dave and the little boy. I hope Dave found love and happiness again. And I pray someone engrained into the little boy's heart that he had a mother who loved him very much and never planned to leave him.

SONG 9 –

THE DEATH OF A DREAM

Not every death is a physical death. Divorce. Failure. Fire. Flood. Moves. End of employment. Growing apart from a friend. Poor health. The dying of a dream.

I was twelve years old when I first realized that I would have a life of service to God and to the church. This realization came as a call to be a missionary.

My home church was participating in a "School of Missions," featuring Baptist missionaries who were at home on furlough from various countries around the world. On one of the nights in the series of meetings, a couple who were not missionaries living "on the foreign field" came to speak. This couple, Lena and Bill, were lay people who, on their own time and at their own expense, traveled around the world visiting Baptist mission work and returned to give presentations on what those missionaries were doing. Lena dressed young people in the clothing she brought home from mission sites, and they displayed objects they called "curios" collected on their trips. They presented a carefully crafted slide program complete with well-written and rehearsed narrative. I saw, heard, and felt things I had never experienced before that evening.

This was years before the internet and before people were traveling as readily as they do now. Going on a trip overseas was a big event that required much planning, expense, and even courage in some cases.

The night Lena and Bill spoke, twelve or fifteen young people in our church assembled ahead of time to be dressed by Lena in garments from different countries and some places in the United States. I wore an exquisite hand-pieced-and-sewn Seminole Indian skirt and poncho. Lena's charm, enthusiasm, smart style, and her almost-like-Minnie-Pearl speech, attracted everyone to her. I was smitten. And it is still my belief that God spoke to me that night as well. For the first time (but not the last), I felt that I was being called to serve God with my life and career. And since the subject that evening was missions, I responded with a commitment to be a missionary.

Let me remind you again that I was only twelve years old. I began a letter correspondence with Lena who nurtured me as a faith mother. Through the years, the call never wavered.

I graduated from college with a degree in music, attended one year of graduate school in music, and then attended and graduated from seminary. I was on my way to becoming a missionary. At age twenty-seven, I was appointed by the mission board to serve in Japan.

My home church and the church in Raleigh of which I was a member at the time were both supportive of me. My friends were proud. Lena and Bill were happy too, though I never felt pressure from them. My widowed mother was supportive of me as well but troubled at the thought of my going so far away for a minimum of four years to a place literally so foreign to her and to me. And, it turns out not surprisingly, she knew me better than I knew myself.

After several months of orientation, I joined ten or eleven other missionaries who were going to Japan at the same time. I was given a lovely apartment in Tokyo. I began to learn my way around and was beginning language school.

Driving was an adventure. Since, in addition to using public transportation, it was going to be necessary at times to drive, there was little choice about the matter. A couple of the seasoned missionaries helped me gain confidence behind the wheel on the "wrong side" of the road, and off I went on my own. One day I ventured out alone to the grocery store a few miles from my apartment. On the way home, I had to drive by the colossal Olympic stadium in the heart of Tokyo. Before I realized what was happening, I was facing an oncoming line of tour buses in *my* lane. But no, in fact, I was in *their* lane. I laugh now to remember how I prayed, "Please, God, don't let me die right here!"

The other new missionaries were settling in, and the career missionaries were lovely but, try as I might, I could not overcome the crippling homesickness I was feeling. I talked and talked to the more experienced missionaries, and they counseled me. I telephoned Lena, and I telephoned Mama, and like me, they too became miserable, not to mention the high cost of those lengthy collect phone calls. Finally, I decided there was no answer except for me to give up and go home.

When I arrived home, I was exhausted and embarrassed. Most people did not know what to say. They tried to be helpful and were maybe even secretly relieved. But it was not enough.

In addition to suffering extreme jetlag for several days, I became depressed. I had no money, no car, no place to live except with my mother, no job, and no good excuses for what had happened. A good friend, the daughter of my mother's neighbor, was in the middle of a divorce after a short marriage, and I felt the close comparison very keenly. The loss of my dream was shattering. And on top of that, I felt that God had somehow jerked the rug out from under me. After all, we had had a bargain. Invitation and response. Call and commitment. My life up in smoke, or so it seemed.

After a few weeks, I knew I had to do *something*. I needed to get a job and a car, and I had to make my way back into life. For a while, I stayed in the nice basement apartment of a friend's house in Raleigh where the hospitality was warm and loving. But there was much spiritual and emotional darkness. I felt as though I was staring down a long, dark tunnel. At times, I did not want to live. The only saving grace was a small, steady light I could see far away at the end of the tunnel. It was, I knew, the love of those who cared deeply for me.

One Wednesday evening, I decided I wanted to go to church; I needed to go to church. The minister who had served for many years at Forest Hills Baptist Church in Raleigh, and whom I had known well, had retired during my time away. A gentleman I did not know was serving there as interim minister until a new permanent minister could be found.

I had a plan. I would arrive a few minutes late to the small chapel where the service was to be held, and I would slip out a few minutes early so I would not have to speak to anyone. The first part of the plan worked, but the second part failed. As the minister was wrapping up his meditation, he said, "There is someone here tonight who needs our special love. I would like to ask Phyllis Mayo to come up here with me for a minute." Shame and dread washed over me as I was thinking, "You don't even know me. Don't do this to me!"

But being an obedient person, I joined him. He slipped his arm around my shoulder and spoke the most life-affirming and grace-filled words that have ever been spoken on my behalf. "This young lady went to Japan as a missionary and now she has come home to you. Some of you know that my wife, Nell, and I were missionaries in Brazil. We came home. But there were missionaries in Brazil who were not supposed to be there, who did not want to be there, but they were too embarrassed, too ashamed of what others would think to come home. This young woman has had the courage to do just that, and you need to love and support her."

There is life in the midst of the death of a dream. Dr. Malcolm Tolbert taught me that lesson on a Wednesday night.

SONG 10 –

THE FISH MAN

In the mid-1970s, the Calhoun and Sarah Johnson family came breezing into the town where I attended college as though riding on the breath of the Holy Spirit. Calhoun, Sarah, and their high school/ early college age children Mia, Philip, Evan, Amy, and Daniel were unlike anyone, anything my friends and I had experienced. Fresh off the mission field in South America, they brought teaching, music, and hospitality to high school and college students in the area. On Saturday nights, their house was jammed with hordes of students who joined in with Phillip, Mia, Evan, and Amy as they played guitars and sang folk-style Christian songs. Calhoun was an enthusiastic teacher, offering the gathered young people fresh ways of living lives of devotion and faith in God. Sarah was the epitome of hospitality as she opened her heart, home, and kitchen to this mob. Sweet-spirited Daniel, the youngest, participated as well.

Leaving the mission work in South America was not a choice they wanted to make, but instead was one they found necessary to make. Daniel, as the story went, got sick with some sort of virus and woke up one morning profoundly deaf. And so, the family came to Wilson, North Carolina, where Daniel could attend the well-regarded school for deaf students with a view to having as normal a life as possible.

Thirty years or more passed. People scattered. And then one evening as I sat eating and visiting with friends in a small, motel restaurant in the mountains of North Carolina, a man came to my table asking, "Are you Phyllis Mayo?" "Yes," I replied, taking a long, hard look at this person who had recognized me, he said, by hearing my voice. It was Philip Johnson. What a happy reunion we had as we caught each other up to date on our activities, and especially those of his family. Calhoun had died some years earlier, but the rest of the family was well and happy.

Another seven or eight years had passed when I read in the newspaper obituaries that a Daniel Johnson had died. Could this be the Daniel I knew? As I continued to read, I found that indeed it was. He had been living in that same college town, serving as minister to the deaf at one of the larger churches there. The funeral was to be held the next day at 6:00 p.m. I determined that I could leave work and drive there, arriving just in time for the service.

The church parking lot was full when I drove in just a couple of minutes past 6:00. I quickly parked and hurried into the large, wide sanctuary. The service had begun, so I found a spot about three rows from the back of the church and slipped into a pew. In a matter of moments, I realized I was surrounded by a sea of deaf people and a few people scattered among them as interpreters. It was fascinating to be there and watch as they enthusiastically but silently communicated with each other. Obviously, Daniel had a large ministry, had touched a lot of lives, and was greatly beloved.

As the service was concluding, it was announced that the family would remain at the front of the sanctuary in order to greet friends. I moved as quickly as I could from the pew and made my way toward the family, wanting to offer my condolences and briefly reconnect in memory of Daniel and of good days past. Even in the midst of their grief, the family radiated God's Spirit of love. Sarah, much aged by now, remembered me, as did the others.

Having shared my words of love and thanksgiving, I began making my way once again through the milling throng of people. Moving toward the back of the church, suddenly I was stopped in my tracks by an unmistakable odor emanating from a man who stood in my path. He smelled like fish. Looking at him, the monogrammed badge on his smeared white work clothes confirmed that he worked at the local fish market.

This man, whom I believe was one of Daniel's flock, had come directly from work, as had I. But he came with something I did not have. He came with the aroma of Christ. I met the fish man, a modern-day Jesus-fisher-in-flesh, who had come from his work of cleaning fish to say good-bye, to say, "Well done, good and faithful servant. I have called you friend."

SONG 11 -

BEARING AWAY

My oldest niece, Susan, married for the second time when her daughters, Summer and Hannah, were ages ten and nine. Her new husband, Justin, marrying for the first time and several years younger than Susan, had a steep learning curve to successfully find his way into the marriage. But soon the girls loved Justin as much as Susan did and were calling him Daddy J.

As comes with the territory of most marriages, Justin also had to make his way into our big, boisterous family. My two sisters and I, their spouses, children and grandchildren, two grandparents, another aunt and uncle, and, on occasion, other special friends, make every effort to get together for birthday celebrations, huge, chaotic holiday meals, graduation parties, and baby showers, and for the traditional yearly homecoming service at church. Justin embraced our traditions, our family, and our unique "craziness," and was soon liked, then loved, by all of us.

Church has always been important in my generation of the family. Maybe not quite as much so in the next generations, but still a part of our family's life. However, for some reason, I began to take notice of Justin as he explored this part of our lives and began to find his own place of comfort. There were times, when I was visiting from out of town, that Justin was at church with Susan and the girls, and once or twice, Justin was there without them. Something was going on in his heart and head. He was finding his way to God, I thought.

After several years of marriage with the usual ups and downs, Justin began having annoying then severe back pain. Different avenues of treatment were explored, but then came a diagnosis of aggressive cancer. This tall, strapping young man began a quick decline. Treatments were tried but nothing was helping. How sad we all felt.

When Justin's pain became unmanageable, he had to be hospitalized. I kept up daily with his condition through my sister Barbara, his mother-in-law. Then one day, in the middle of the afternoon, she called me at work. "Susan wants Justin to be baptized before he dies. He's changing fast but he is still aware of what's going on. Can you come right now?"

My only brief question was, "Does Justin want this?" When Barbara replied that he did, I grabbed my Bible, another book, a bowl, my purse, and flew out of my office to drive the fifty minutes to the hospital. I prayed and sought God's guidance as I drove. I prayed I would not get stopped for speeding. I prayed Justin would not die before I arrived at the hospital. But most of all, I prayed that I would know the right things to say and would be guided to do my best to offer not only the sacrament of Holy Baptism but comfort and love as well.

When I got to the floor of the hospital near Justin's room, the hallway and the waiting area were crammed with our family. Everyone who could get there was there, including not only Susan's side of the family but also Justin's parents, and his sister who had flown in from out of state the day before. I had met his family at the wedding several years prior but knew virtually nothing about their lives.

Susan was in the room but came out in the hall to speak with me. I asked her again if baptism was what Justin wanted and she confirmed this. Then she invited me into the room.

Justin lay in the hospital bed, body swollen, chest heaving with every breath, unable to speak, but alert. His mother and father, his sister, and Susan, Summer, and Hannah, were present. The small, dimly lit room felt very much like the sanctuary it had become for them.

I approached Justin's side. I told him I did not expect him to talk but did want him to answer one question for me if he could. "Do you want to be baptized?" He vigorously nodded his head, "Yes."

On the drive to the hospital, as I had sought from God the right words to say in such a difficult time, I was reminded of the story of Jesus, a paralyzed man, and his friends, as told in the Gospel of Luke. As the story goes, a large crowd had gathered inside and outside someone's home where Jesus was teaching and healing many people. The paralyzed man's friends carried him there on a mat but were unable to maneuver their way through the crowd. Ingeniously, they devised another way to access Jesus. They removed tiles from the roof and, using ropes, lowered the man on the mat through the opening literally to the feet of Jesus.

As I prepared for Justin's baptism, I invited his gathered family to do the same for him. Unable to have conversation with the minister of a church, to walk down a church aisle, to confess his sins, to be baptized in a church, Justin had, nevertheless, made it known he wished to be baptized. And the only way to accomplish this was for his family to bring him to the feet of Jesus.

I handed to Justin's father a small bowl I had purchased in a shop by the Sea of Galilee. Water from the hospital room faucet was poured into the bowl. Then, standing by Justin's side, I turned to the family. I told them the story of the paralyzed man, of his friends bearing him to Christ for healing. I reminded them that on this day, Justin would not be healed in body but would indeed be healed in spirit.

I then turned to Justin and spoke words of God's love for him. Once again, he nodded his head in confirmation. Then, with Justin's father holding the bowl of water and his family bearing him to Jesus, I prayed, dipped my finger into the now-holy water, crossed Justin's forehead with the sign of the cross, and kissed him on the cheek, committing him to God's eternal care.

SONG 12 –

SERENDIPITY

When I was a child, Mr. Roy and "Miss" Judy lived next door to us. There was barely an alleyway between our houses and, because there was no air conditioning in those days, in warm weather sounds could be heard from our windows to theirs. Though I was only three or four years old, I was always singing, and since they could hear me from next door, Roy and Judy (or Miss Jukie, as I mispronounced her name) called me Ethel Merman.

They had no children and were especially adoring of the three girls in our family. They had a big place in my heart too.

One vivid memory is of Judy and Mama sitting on the back porch preparing vegetables to make relish. Since I apparently believed that I was not getting enough attention, I decided to stuff a pea-sized stone up my nose. Though with some gentle nose-blowing, no crisis ensued, I got a little extra attention, along with a good scolding.

When I was in first grade, our family moved to a new town, then Judy and Roy moved as well. But thanks to the tradition of sending Christmas cards, my mother and Judy kept in touch. I even remember a few visits with them over the years.

Many years passed. I was in my late twenties, and one night I dreamed about Judy. So being an adult now, I decided it was okay for me to phone them. Fully expecting the lady of the house to answer the phone, I was a little thrown off balance when a man's voice answered. I asked for "Miss Judy." It was Roy who answered, and he very gently told me she had died a couple of years earlier. I was shaken to say the least. After all those years, I dreamed about her, wished to talk with her, and then learned she had died.

Very graciously, Roy followed up the phone call with a letter to me. He explained what had happened to Judy, how much he missed her, and how he remembered so fondly our days as neighbors. We sent Christmas cards for a few years, then the correspondence tapered off.

More time passed, and I was working at Springmoor Retirement Community in Raleigh. Alice and Amy were two never-married sisters who had come to live there. By the time of their move, their only remaining family consisted of two nephews and two nieces, all of whom lived out of town. As the chaplain, I spent a lot of time with the sisters, as one of them was terminally ill, and I just plain liked their spunk. Over the course of many conversations, I learned about the nephews and nieces but had not met them. Then came a delightful surprise.

As I walked down the hall one day, I saw an older man and woman going in the door of the chapel, which was not far from my office. I stopped dead in my tracks, knowing without a doubt that I had just seen Roy. Though it had been many years since I had seen him, he was undeniably the same Roy I had known as a child. (Loving people make lasting impressions on young children.) I followed him into the chapel and sputtered, "Do you know who I am?" As one might expect, he looked at me completely unknowing. "I'm Phyllis Mayo. What in the world are you doing here?" Shocked as I was, and still getting his wits about him, Roy explained that his niece (actually Judy's niece) had come to visit her two aunts, who as it turned out were my two friends, Alice and Amy. He and his new wife had come along to give the niece some company on the drive from out of town. The niece, whom I had not met before this day, was the spitting image of Judy, her voice especially. This chance encounter was almost unbelievable. The two sisters . . . a visiting niece . . . a now long-deceased friend . . . a remarried husband. Had I been thirty seconds earlier or later walking down the hall, I would have missed Roy altogether.

By the time this wonderful serendipity happened, both my parents had died as well. I wanted so badly to call my mother and tell her what had happened, whom I had seen, but I did not need to do that. My only thought, the vision so clear in my mind, was of Judy and Mama, together in heaven, tapping me on the shoulder and shouting, "Hey Phyllis, hey Phyllis, that's Roy! Don't miss him!" What rejoicing in heaven and on earth!

SONG 13 –

HANDS

I stood outside the door to her room for several minutes before knocking. I took deep breaths not knowing what I would find, what condition I would witness. She was terminally ill, and I had not yet met her.

Knock, knock. "May I come in?" A big smile and "Bonjour!" greeted me. Though not French, Hazel was speaking French to me. And on top of that, she whipped off her cloth turban to show me her bald head. It took no time for me to breathe easy and release any fears that had come with me to her door. She was charming. I was captivated.

Only months prior, Hazel had been diagnosed with a brain tumor. As it had become more and more challenging for her to remain in her home, her brother, who lived a hundred miles away, and some Raleigh friends moved her to Springmoor. Since I was still the social worker at that time, she became "mine" too. When we had received the pre-admission information on her, she had been given only two to three months to live. Wrong.

Margaret, a piano teacher like Hazel and her closest friend, came almost daily to visit. As I got to know Margaret, she told me the back story of Hazel's life. As it turned out, we had three major slices of life in common: we were both music majors in college; we were both never-married women; and we were not morning people.

I visited Hazel in her room usually five days a week. Since her remaining time was expected to be short, I wanted to get to know her and for her to know me. But her time went beyond the expected. The director of nursing chastised me for spending too much time with her, afraid I would "take it too hard when she died." I paid no attention to her. I was doing as I would want someone to do for me.

There were ups and downs with Hazel's health. At times, we thought the beginning of the end was near. Then there would be long periods when she seemed to be doing better. Of course, better did not mean well. For a while she could walk just a few steps with a lot of assistance, and then none at all. But she could entertain us with her sassy ways and her sometimes salty tongue.

As I spent more and more time with her, as months passed by and became well over a year, I developed deep feelings for Hazel. She had lived a successful, independent life as a single woman, and I had high respect for that. She was a fun person, and I liked that. But she was also dying, and that made me sad. At first, I was only visiting. Then I began to help feed her. And finally, there came a time when she would not take medicine from the nurses unless I encouraged her. My newly found friend was slipping away bit by bit.

Often as I sat by her bed and talked, I would hold her hand, a hand that years before had been badly broken in a fall and repaired with slightly bent fingers so she could still play piano. I felt that I was offering support to her, and she gave every indication that she enjoyed having me there.

The time came when Hazel was no longer able to express herself verbally, but still I talked. She got quite ill, so much so that we thought her death was imminent, but once more she bounced back. Later as I was talking to her, holding her hand, I said, "Hazel, we thought you were dying. Margaret and I stayed here and were with you." And to my everlasting memory, she was haltingly able to reply, "Your holding my hand was what kept me here."

When Margaret told me that Hazel was not a morning person, she quoted her as saying, "I don't even want to die in the morning!" But she did. And on a Saturday morning at that. A day any working single woman might want to sleep late.

Hazel and I were never able to have conversation about her faith, though I do believe she found God in music and in her friends. One day I will hold her bent-fingered hand again, and we will talk. But for now, I know that my hands cannot keep someone here with me forever, no matter how special the person is, no matter how much I love them. God's own hands of love are enough for now and for eternity.

SONG 14 –

A PARTING GIFT FOR MOTHER

Mary Kelley moved to Springmoor as an adult in the care of her mother and father. Her father, a gentle soul, was a retired minister. He had suffered many years of tenuous health and died after they had been at Springmoor only a few years. Her mother was brilliant, tough, and in charge. Had she been born a generation or two later, she would have held her own alongside any male minister. Instead, she was a social worker, a scholarly Bible teacher, and the only person who could truly meet the needs of Mary Kelley.

Mary Kelley had, all her adult life, suffered mental illness. Awkward in appearance, she nevertheless had a winning personality. Her big smile and friendly greeting belied what was underneath, stirring in her troubled mind. Yet she had the best life her parents, together with her brothers and her sister, could give her.

At Springmoor, Mary Kelley and her mother found true pleasure in singing with the HotShots, a group of resident singers. They wore fun hats and sang familiar, light-hearted songs. Their programs were greatly entertaining, even garnering for them occasional invitations to sing in other communities or at church events. As a member of this group, Mary Kelley was just like everyone else, flowered hat, calico skirt, and all.

As with many, many mothers of children with disabilities, adult or otherwise, Mary Kelley's mother wanted nothing more than to out-live Mary Kelley. That was not to be.

The family gathered by her bedside as she was dying. Hymns had played a prominent role in the life of this worshiping family, and as this mother lay dying familiar hymns played in the room all day. But the most precious gift of those last moments came from Mary Kelley. She sat by "Mother's" bed, talked to her, expressed her love . . . and sweetly sang her home.

SONG 15 –

CUDDLING

When Eleanor and Max moved to Springmoor, neither of them was well. Eleanor was already deeply ravaged by Alzheimer's disease, and Max, it turned out, had advanced cancer. They both moved into the health care center but had separate rooms, since their care needs were so different.

During this period, I was in a part-time master's degree program and was working all kinds of odd hours to maintain full-time status in my job as social worker for the health center.

And so it was that a bittersweet moment presented itself for Max, Eleanor, and me.

As I sat at the nurses' station going on toward ten o'clock one evening working on patient charts, Max was sitting alone in a dark corner of the TV lounge area adjacent to where I was working. I decided to take a break to visit with him.

"You're up mighty late this evening," I said, reaching out a hand to him. He greeted me kindly and replied that he was "just thinking," glad, I thought, to have a little company.

I guessed that he was thinking about Eleanor, asleep down the hall in her semi-private room. I realized, too, that his impending death must surely be on his mind. So I asked if he would like to go in and spend a while with Eleanor to say good night. "Yes, that would be nice," he replied with a smile.

I rolled him down the hall to her room and placed his wheelchair as close to Eleanor's bed as possible so he could whisper to her and hold her hand. Leaving the two of them there, I told him I would come back in a while to get him.

When I returned about thirty minutes later, Max had a request. "I would like to spend the night in bed with my wife." I consulted with the nursing supervisor, and we both agreed this would not disturb the roommate, also an Alzheimer's patient, and would be a lovely moment for Max and Eleanor.

Max and Eleanor were both tall and quite thin. The nurse and I moved Eleanor over to one side of the bed, making sure the bedrail was up for safety, and then we lifted Max into bed with her. "Eleanor, Max is coming to bed now." "Mm, hmm," she naturally acknowledged. The single bed, both rails up, provided just enough room for them to cuddle for the night.

Max was most grateful. He died with great peace just a few days later.

Their three sons and daughter were faithful visitors. But the daughter was especially touched by the story of her parents' last night together. She wrote a note to me, expressing all the thanks she could put into words. The note was written on a carefully selected card on which two teddy bears sat in a window, arms wrapped around each other, looking out at the moon. I saw the daughter again on several occasions, and she never failed to thank me for that precious night of cuddling, that night of peace and love, that night of tender "see you again soon" for her mom and dad.

SONG 16 –
THE RECEIVING

Sawyer was two years and two days old when a devastating accident took away any and all chances he had of surviving to fully know and experience the life and love his parents and grandparents had dreamed of for him. Because of the nature of the accident which left him brain-dead but still breathing with assistance, his vital organs were deemed viable for transplant. And that is what his brave, loving, selfless, broken-hearted parents decided to do. Several lives were saved because his life, as it had been, ended.

I knew Sawyer's maternal great-grandmother and maternal grandmother, and had met Sawyer once or twice with his mother. He was a beautiful and sweet child with a brother just two years older than he.

Because I knew him and had the relationship with his maternal line, I was asked to speak about Sawyer at the funeral. On a warm, sunny afternoon I met for about three hours with his parents on the patio in the backyard of his paternal grandparents' home. They talked and talked about him, about his personality, how precious he was to all the family, and things that have now long since faded from my memory.

I prepared to speak at the funeral and am guessing now that I repeated much of what his parents had told me. And surely, I must have talked about the invaluable gifts of life generously endowed to the patients, together with their families, who received transplanted organs from Sawyer's little body. But I honestly do not remember exactly what I said. It was almost more than I could even imagine to be standing in the pulpit of the crowded church saying anything at all that might comfort Sawyer's family and the throng of people who mourned so deeply.

As the pastor of the church led the main parts of the service that day, he was charged with "explaining God" by giving the sermon, by trying to justify the ever-watchful, never-failing love of God with His seeming failure to protect or save Sawyer, this innocent child. Yet this inspiring man said words I shall never forget, words I hope others will remember as well: "*We ask questions when such a time as this comes. Chief among all the big questions we ask is 'Why? Why would God take a child in such a tragic way?' Let me assure you that God did not take Sawyer. No, God did not take Sawyer. The laws of nature say that when such an accident happens, a person will die. But God did not do this. God did not take Sawyer. Here is what happened. Because an accident happened, because Sawyer could no longer live, because Sawyer died, God received him.*"

After the funeral at the church, I went to the cemetery to help the family bury their beloved son, brother, grandson. I stopped between the church and the cemetery and purchased a half dozen or so little-boy-blue balloons. Family members released them heavenward, and we watched them drift away, blue into blue. And God received Sawyer.

SONG 17 –

LIKE HOLLAND IN THE SPRINGTIME

Sisters Alice and Amy lived together all their adult lives in a mid-sized town where they had satisfying jobs and great friends. Alice worked as a buyer for a chain of stores, and Amy worked in the office of a bank president. Neither of them married, and I never heard either of them speak of serious gentleman friends, though that could have been a part of their lives they did not divulge.

They moved fifty or so miles to Springmoor after Alice had suffered through some serious illnesses. They were wise women who knew how to plan for future needs and how to make the most of the remaining years of their lives.

In their hometown, they claimed a group of female friends with whom they shared many good times and much enjoyment. Self-named "the Unclaimed Jewels," all the women in the group knew they were well worth the salt and bone of which they were made. They had happy personalities and contented lives. For Alice and Amy, this lifestyle continued at Springmoor as they made countless friends, including lucky me.

The two-bedroom apartment they shared was modern, old South. Every piece of furniture, every flower, every pillow, every figurine, every magazine, was perfect and in its place. Visiting them was like a real-life version of visiting the Baldwin sisters from *The Waltons*, minus the "recipe," at least for the chaplain. They were fun, hospitable, and genuinely loving to me and all their friends.

Because her hair had thinned with chemotherapy, Alice wore a cute little wig. A stroke slowed her walking somewhat, but she dressed to impress. Her deep brown eyes and her wit carried her along as a force to be reckoned with. Amy was very petite. When people (impolitely) commented on her small size (Why do people find it okay to comment on a person's "smallness" but not their "fatness?"), Amy would rear her shoulders back, straighten her back, proudly lift her head, and retort, "I'm as big as I can be!" That shut them up.

In November 1988, at one o'clock in the morning when an F-4 tornado destroyed a K-Mart and many homes and took two lives, its fury raged within a half mile of Springmoor, flattening a church within sight of Alice and Amy's apartment. The wind tore shingles and sheeting from the roof of their building, and rain poured in, but the worst of the inside damage was in Alice and Amy's apartment. A board crashed through a picture window, impaling the dropped leaf of their dining table. Not five minutes earlier, Amy had walked through the room directly by the table. The ceiling of the apartment was sucked down low enough that it could be touched with little effort by raising one's hand above one's head. Near catastrophic yet causing no bodily harm, it nevertheless unnerved Amy and Alice. But, being resilient women of faith, they bravely soldiered through.

Alice had cancer and a stroke before the move to Springmoor, and eventually the two conditions reared their heads again. When she was no longer able to stay in the apartment, she moved to the health care center on campus, where Amy visited for hours each day. Never ones to be glum, they entertained me on my frequent visits. In fact, they decided to "adopt" me. I was, by their invitation, to call them "Big Sister," and they were going to call me "Little Sister," that is until Amy considered the fact that I weighed about what the two of them combined weighed. My name, thus, was changed to "Baby Sister."

As Alice's condition grew more troublesome, it became appropriate for her to receive occasional painkillers. One Friday evening, I was at home. I had cooked and eaten a nice dinner when I got a call saying that perhaps I should come in to be with Alice because her breathing had changed. When I arrived, her breaths were indeed quite diminished. Amy had not yet arrived. I leaned over Alice and began talking to her, trying to soothe her in the event these were her dying moments.

The dinner I had prepared for myself that evening was heavy with garlic, so I slapped a big piece of gum in my mouth on the drive over. Now at her bedside as I continued talking lovingly and gently to "sleeping" Alice, she suddenly perked up and said, "Get out of my face with that garlic breath. That gum's not helping a bit!" The drugs, it seemed, had slowed her breathing to a more comfortable level so she had been resting well, until I came along with garlic breath. She did not die that night or for several months to come.

I spent many hours with these two loving sisters, some fun times and some more serious. Once I asked Alice what she thought heaven would be like, and without missing a beat, and flashing her deep, dark eyes at me, she said, "Like Holland in the springtime."

I do not remember the particular moment of Alice's death nor Amy's a few years later, but I see them now enjoying a perpetual Holland springtime.

SONG 18 –
A FEATHER IN HER HAIR

My Springmoor friend, Barbara, could be described as part hippie, part bohemian, very fashion-forward, and always elegant. She managed to pull off that combination of style and demeanor without a thought, though I think she would be most delighted to be called a hippie. Tall and statuesque, she wore long skirts, and Birkenstocks, which she pronounced in the German, "beer-kin-schtock." She had toenails polished bright yellow or green before teenage girls were doing it. And when it became a "thing" to put a streak of color in one's hair for breast cancer awareness, she had a stripe of pink added to her blond hair. My favorite, however, was the thin red feather she had woven into her hair for a few months. I envied her joie de vivre and her guts to live it out in a big way.

Her first marriage was to a man who, from her description, was a looker and a charmer. I could picture the two of them together as a striking couple. When that marriage ended with his death, Barbara started a whole new life as an independent woman by moving to Germany where she taught English.

An old beau, one she almost married in college, found her, and traveled to Germany to woo her back home. She delighted in telling the story of him swinging his fraternity pin on a gold chain back and forth in front of her face to hypnotize her to "come home and marry me." It worked. She did.

When they moved to Springmoor, Barbara's husband was already beginning to have some health issues, and after a while needed to move into the health care facility. He died after a year or so. I still remember the simple, tasteful navy-blue dress she wore to his memorial service.

Barbara enjoyed life at Springmoor where she made friends laugh, including me. When she began to have some walking challenges, she purchased a scooter on which to ride up and down the long halls. It was a doozy . . . larger, more equipped, and "blinged-out" than most of the others in the hallways, and it was Barbara all the way.

Barbara told wonderful stories of her childhood.

When she was about ten years old, a friend invited her to a party, but it was not just any party. The guest of honor was First Lady Eleanor Roosevelt. The large lawn party was to be held at the home of her friend's parents. Barbara's mother got busy finding the right dress for her to wear, and most especially, making sure her daughter was schooled in how to greet Mrs. Roosevelt. She was to curtsy and say, "Only in a country such as ours could a little girl like I be privileged to meet the wife of the President." Things went off without a hitch. Mrs. Roosevelt smiled and patted her on the head. On telling the story, which she must have told many times in her life, with laughter, Barbara recalled noticing Mrs. Roosevelt's big teeth as she looked up and her big feet as she looked down.

Soon Barbara and her friend grew tired of playing outside with the adults, and the friend suggested they go inside to play in her room. They climbed the steps to the second floor of the big house and as they went down the hall, they passed the guest room where Mrs. Roosevelt was staying. There they saw several hats laid out on a bed. They looked up and down the hall and saw no one, so they stepped into the room and began trying on Mrs. Roosevelt's hats in front of the full-length mirror. Then they spotted her shoes. So they slipped their own little-girl feet into her big shoes. As they pranced about, giggling and admiring themselves, they heard someone coming. Quickly, oh so quickly, they put the hats and shoes back in place without getting caught and escaped to the friend's room in the nick of time. Whew!

Barbara remained full of life up to the end. One day I received an urgent call saying that she was hospitalized and was asking for me to come. I got there in short order and visited Barbara with her daughters and son-in-law in the intensive care unit. She had developed a problem that needed immediate surgical attention, but there was no guarantee she would survive. Barbara and her trusted family were grappling with a decision about surgery. I told her how much I loved her and enjoyed her friendship. I knew Barbara wanted me to pray with all those gathered, so I asked them for their own specifics for prayer. Barbara answered. So alert, so aware of her situation, so tenderly she said, "I'm a little bit afraid." Holding her hand, I prayed that she and her beloved family would find peace. She died a short time later, in peace, without fear.

I do not believe Barbara would especially like a halo. "Too shiny," she'd say. But I do expect, one day, to see her again with a slender red feather in her hair.

SONG 19 –

THE YARDSTICK AND THE ROPE

Laura and Joe were a loving, happy, friendly couple. When they entered a room, everyone noticed—for more than one reason. First and foremost, they always had big smiles and were warm to everyone, and second, Laura leaned heavily on Joe to walk.

Laura had developed some type of neurological disease before their move to Springmoor, and like many of those diseases, it was, unfortunately, progressive. Still they maintained their positive demeanor despite what was gradually but obviously happening to her.

They attended one of the small groups I led, making an effort to always be there. Joe thought it was important to keep Laura involved, to give her opportunities to be heard rather than just seen, and to have her experience the affection of those who were her friends and neighbors.

I was on vacation when I received a call that Joe had died suddenly. I returned home and had the privilege of conducting the memorial service for this exceedingly fine, caring man.

Their story, a funny and poignant one, was happily shared by their son as part of Joe's eulogy:

Nothing epitomized [Dad's] devotion to Mom better and more humorously than during a trip to Gardner-Webb University for Sarah's graduation. We arranged for Mom and Dad to have a handicap suite in the new motel in Boiling Springs. We all laughed that it looked more like a honeymoon suite than handicap because it had a gas log fireplace and Jacuzzi tub. As we moved the suitcases and other travel items into the room, Mom and Dad looked at the two double beds and looked each other. Mom asked Dad in a quiet tone, "Did you bring the rope?" All of us in the room stopped cold and said, "ROPE?" Dad's simple response was, "Sure, you know I have to help your mother to the bathroom at night and when we don't have a king or queen size bed, we sleep separately. If it is too far for her to hit me with the yard stick we carry, I tie a rope to my ankle and over to the bed post for Laura to pull when she needs me." There was a moment of silence, and we all burst out laughing!

Laura, of course, needed to move into the health care facility on the Springmoor campus after Joe's death. His unfailing love and the tremendous support he provided were now gone. By this time, Laura's abilities had decreased greatly, including her ability to speak discernably. When I visited her, offering my love, condolences, and prayers, she could acknowledge my presence and words with her eyes only. She lived just a couple of months past Joe's death. I think Joe must have been hitting her with the yardstick or pulling on the rope for Laura to join him.

SONG 20 –
THE PASSAGE

John and Nancy were private people, just the two of them with an exceptionally small family and group of friends, at least as I knew them. John, in his working career, had been a statistician, and Nancy had a career as well, though I do not recall the nature of her work. Perhaps their lives had at one time been more spirited and connected with others, but that was not the case when they came to Springmoor. John was friendly enough one-on-one but interacted with others only within the confines of his apartment. Nancy lived in the health care center.

When they moved to Springmoor, neither of them was well. John ultimately died of lung cancer following a lifetime of smoking, but it is Nancy's death that has informed my "death and dying education" more than most others.

John was still alive but not at all well when Nancy was dying. He was not able to be present at her bedside, so I spent as much time with her as I could spare. As I remember, she was noncommunicative, and so being with her was simply that . . . being with her.

As the days went by, she was in a steady decline but, as I recall, was not suffering. The medical staff made sure she was well cared for and not in pain.

The minutes leading up to her last breaths are fixed solidly and clearly in my mind.

As I sat by her side, Nancy's breathing diminished bit by bit by bit. As her breathing grew more shallow, I knew from many prior experiences that the end was near, but up to this time, there had never, with other patients, been a defining indicator I had observed which spoke to me with absolute clarity, "The last moments of life are upon us, death is near." Over many years, I had sat and watched as the breathing of those who were dying had changed dramatically, from thirty seconds or more of not breathing (apnea) to breaths so shallow as to be barely detectable. In many cases, the families and caregiving staff would wait for hours, or perhaps days, or even weeks for the end to come, when it seemed impossible for life to continue, when all signs pointed to imminent death. And then, with Nancy, everything changed.

As I watched Nancy, suddenly I was taken aback to see a very distinct grimace cross her face as simultaneously she bent her head forward and pulled in her shoulders toward her chest. The corners of her mouth turned downward, as if bearing down, and her eyes tightened into a closed squint. After only seconds, this grimacing ceased, and in moments, her breathing stopped.

I sat there amazed at what I had just seen. It did not appear to be painful. It did not appear to be a struggle. There were no sounds.

Only what appeared to be a push. And then it dawned on me. I had witnessed Nancy's passage through the birth canal from life to death to life.

I have never had children. Nor did Nancy. But on the day Nancy died, we were both present for an amazing, beautiful birth. What she saw after her passage through the birth canal, I have not yet seen. But when I think about transitioning from life to death to life again, I think about being in my own mother's womb being presented with a question. "Do you want to stay here where it is cozy and warm and safe, where you are loved and being fed, or would you like to venture out into a new life filled with wonders you cannot imagine if you stay here?" Though it would be a difficult, perhaps frightening decision and a harrowing journey, I would choose the latter. Always the next adventure. Always life.

Thank you, Nancy, for the most holy and marvelous gift of witnessing your passage.

SONG 21 –

THE THIN LINE

Sally had a stroke about six months before she moved into the health care center at Springmoor. The stroke had left her unable to speak and, by the time we first saw her, she was in a fetal position with clenched hands. The only life-sustaining thing she could do was swallow.

The room Sally occupied had two beds. She was in the first bed nearer the door. Her roommate, in the bed by the window, was a woman who was quite alert and had lived at Springmoor for a few years. I knew her well and visited her at least weekly.

One day as I passed by Sally's bed, giving her a look of pity but no real attention, it occurred to me that she too was a human being, deserving of all the attention and care I could give her. She had a daughter, and a grandson with developmental disabilities, who visited her as much as possible, but this left her just lying there most of the day with little conversation directed to her except by those who were meeting her physical caregiving needs.

I decided to talk with her daughter to learn more about Sally. As it turned out, we were members of the same church. She had had the stroke before I became active there, so I had not known her at church, but I knew someone who would have known her. Mrs. Kelly, a long-time church member, was not only the church librarian but also unofficial historian-archivist-picture-taker. When there was an event other than the regular Sunday worship service, Mrs. Kelly was there with her camera.

I went to Mrs. Kelly and asked her about Sally. It was no tough assignment for her. We went to the church library, and she immediately began pulling out picture albums, one after the other. As we thumbed through them, she helped me find some good photos of Sally. With a promise of returning them safely, I asked if I might borrow them to take to Sally's room. Mrs. Kelly was more than delighted to accommodate me.

Thus began my real journey with Sally.

I took the photo albums to my office, and one at the time, as often as I had opportunity, I took them to her room. Since I knew a good number of people in the pictures, I would turn the pages one by one and tell Sally who I was seeing and the church activities in which they were engaged. She made no response, but I persisted. I talked and talked as though we were having a two-way conversation but, in reality, had no idea if she was hearing or comprehending anything I was saying.

It was especially nice to look at the pictures of Sally, seeing her when she was well and active. I told her daughter what I was doing, and she was most appreciative. I was growing to love Sally, though I had never seen her walk, use her hands, heard her voice speak or laugh, and detected no true eye to eye communication between us.

Each time I visited, I tried to help her feel like a real person, the real person she had been and still was in some ways. But, again, I had no idea if any of this was making even the slightest difference for Sally.

One day, after several weeks of regular visits, as it was time for me to end our visit, I kissed her on the cheek, and said, "Bye, Sally. May I come again soon?" And to my absolute astonishment, she said very clearly, "You certainly may."

I was thrilled beyond description and raced to the phone to call her daughter. When she answered, I exclaimed, "You won't believe this, but your mother is talking!" It had been more than six months since she had spoken a single word. The daughter was as dumbfounded as I and came over as soon as she could.

Sally talked for about six weeks and then she stopped again. But we knew by then that she was still there, still a vital soul in a damaged body.

I do not remember much about Sally's death, but I clearly remember the day she crossed the thin line back to life.

SONG 22 –

SECRETS AMONG FRIENDS

Dottie, Evelyn, and Margaret had known each other for decades. They, together with their husbands, had been members of the same Sunday school class for forty or fifty years. Dottie and Bernard, Evelyn and Charles, Margaret and Chet, and two or three other couples were young marrieds when their friendship began. This group of couples shared the excitement of having children and the challenges of rearing them. They went in and out of each other's homes like family. They shared recipes and meals, birthdays and holidays, and work projects. They went through hard times and good times together, forming strong bonds of friendship and love. They watched their children grow up, get married, have children and grandchildren of their own. They attended church as faithfully as any people ever did. They teamed up on church committees and in life, carrying each other along as only dear, trusted friends can do.

Dottie and Bernard moved to Springmoor first and were there several years before Bernard died after a brief illness. Already living at Springmoor, Chet died suddenly one evening while sitting on the sofa beside Margaret. Charles and Evelyn were contemplating a move to Springmoor when Charles, too, died quite unexpectedly. Evelyn moved shortly thereafter.

Eventually all three women lived in the health care center: Margaret on the first floor, Evelyn and Dottie on the second floor. Each of them had memory deficits, enough that they could no longer safely live independently, yet not robbing them of their ability to communicate. Since I was a member of the same church and had known them fifteen or twenty years, I could have facilitated with the three of them a conversation about the "old days," and they would, for the most part, have been able to participate. But as it was, they were unable to seek out each other and have such conversations on their own. I suspect their daughters did get them together on occasion.

Evelyn began a sharp decline in physical health in addition to her mental decline. One of her daughters died, and she was unaware of her absence. Then Evelyn died.

I was with the remaining daughter in Evelyn's room at the time of her death and stayed until the funeral home representatives arrived to remove her body.

A short time later, as I walked down the hall, I saw Dottie sitting in her wheelchair near the nurses' station. I stopped and told the nurses that I was going to tell Dottie about Evelyn's death, since they had been such close friends for so many years. I pulled up a chair beside Dottie and sat down. Trying to find the easiest way to tell Dottie that her friend had died, I said, "Hi, Dottie. Did you hear about Evelyn?" Immediately she replied, "Yes. She's pregnant, but it's a secret. She's not telling anyone yet."

The nurses who heard this, their mouths agape and their eyes bugging out, nearly fell off their chairs, trying not to laugh, and I had to fight hard to maintain my composure. Then I told Dottie that Evelyn had died, did my best to offer her comfort, and made my way downstairs.

When I got downstairs, who was sitting right there in front of me but Margaret. "Well," I thought, "I need to tell Margaret too." Having learned my lesson, I took a different approach this time. As gently as I could, I told her that Evelyn had died. She calmly and sweetly replied, "We had such good times together."

Indeed, they did. Indeed, they did. In life, in death, and in the secrets of new life to come.

SONG 23 –

IN LIFE, IN DEATH, IN LIFE

Alice was a sharp, active, self-aware woman when she moved to Springmoor as one of the earliest residents. She was divorced and had established a solid and satisfying life for herself. She had a great relationship with her daughter, her grandchildren, and, oddly, it seemed to me, her ex-husband. She was a women's libber. She promoted anything and everything that would give women a voice in the world. She had a happy personality, a quick smile, and brought joy to those who knew her.

I convened a group meeting twice a month for discussion of various topics, and Alice regularly attended. A woman of faith, she shocked me and others in the group by saying she was a member of the Hemlock Society. She would, she said, take her own life if she felt that she was developing profound memory loss. While I struggled to respect her right to follow the course she had committed to take, I prayed it would never be necessary. She made advance arrangements with the Alzheimer's study program of a local hospital for brain donation as a "normal" subject, hoping her mind would stay clear to the end.

Several years passed, and then a man with the same last name as Alice appeared in her life. We soon learned that this man, Ralph, was Alice's ex-husband. She seemed happy, so I concluded it must be okay, until I heard that they were going to remarry. At that point, I admit, I was a bit suspicious of his presence in her life again.

To Alice's great credit, she had never spoken ill of Ralph, at least in my hearing. In fact, she would often say, "He just made a mistake." Oh, to be so forgiving. And by her account, the relationship through the years had been sound enough that, even though for a while he was married to someone else, they jointly traveled out of state to care for their grandchildren while their daughter and her husband took vacations.

So Alice and Ralph remarried, and he moved into Springmoor with her. I quickly learned that I had to take my foot out of my mouth, eat my words, and swallow my pride. I had to admit that not only did I like Ralph, but I found him also to be a true, kind, and gracious gentleman, and ultimately a friend. He and Alice were very happy together.

After several years of marriage, and both advancing in age, each of them encountered medical issues. Alice, as she had feared, did develop dementia. Ralph had cancer which required a fairly radical surgery. But he kept up his spirits and did well for a while, simultaneously making sure he cared for Alice.

Eventually, Ralph's condition deteriorated to the point that he needed to move to the health care center, so it was necessary for Alice to move as well. They occupied the same room until Ralph was too sick for that to work. He worried about her, and she did not completely grasp what was happening to him. To keep them apart but still close,

Alice was moved to a room adjacent to Ralph's. Their daughter came and stayed for several weeks, tenderly caring for both her parents as her father was dying.

I was there with them the night Ralph died. We did all the usual things, such as contacting and waiting for the funeral home to arrive. We brought Alice into the room to say good-bye. And then, after several days, the daughter went back home, out of state.

No more than two or three weeks after Ralph's death, nurses and others began noticing a marked decline in Alice's health. She had not expressed or shown signs of deep grief, and frankly, we were not sure if she fully comprehended what had happened. But she grew sicker and sicker over a couple of weeks, and then she too died.

Alice and Ralph's daughter had returned to be with her mother for her last week or two of life, and I had grown to appreciate her and her family's story very much. She had all the lovely qualities of both her parents.

The night of Alice's death, instead of calling a funeral home, our task was to phone the Alzheimer's research program representative on call and have them arrange for Alice's body to be removed and taken to their facility for study purposes. We made that call, and as we waited a couple of hours, the daughter and I talked and did other necessary chores, including having the nurse retrieve Alice's wedding rings from the safe. As she handed them to the daughter, I remember noticing one wedding ring with a small diamond but no wedding band. "Lost," I thought.

The next day I received a call from Mary, the representative from the Alzheimer's research program. She was trying to phone Alice's daughter but had been unable to reach her. I had seen the daughter shortly before the phone call came and was able to tell Mary where she was and how soon I might be able to contact her. Since this was before cell phones were commonly used, Mary asked me to please get in touch with the daughter and have her call back as soon as possible.

And then Mary said, "We've had the strangest finding on autopsy I've ever seen or heard of. We found Alice's wedding band lodged in the tissue of her lung." Putting together the whole story of her quick decline, we concluded that in her confusion Alice must have some-how aspirated the ring into her lung where it became embedded and caused pneumonia, leading to her death. Since this would have been extremely difficult to achieve on purpose, it was almost certainly an accident, a fluke.

Those of us who received this information did agree, though, that Alice got her wish after all. She did not have to travel the full distance of the often years-long road of dementia. She did not have to take her own life. Instead, she found yet another life, an eternal life with Ralph, the love of her life.

In life, in death, in life.

SONG 24 –

THE TEAR

Mrs. Helms was an educator, spending the last decades of her career as a teacher at North Carolina's Governor Morehead School for the Blind. Although by the time I knew her she had lost so much to dementia, including most of her speech, I could still picture her walking down the halls of the school, commanding respect, garnering admiration, and offering vital instruction. Her husband had died some years before she came to Springmoor. She had one son and a daughter-in-law who were caring and devoted to her. They visited on a regular basis even when she no longer appeared to recognize them. It was clear Mrs. Helms and her husband had nurtured their son in a loving and kind home.

One evening is so clear in my memory. It appeared to the nursing supervisor and to me that Mrs. Helms and the woman in the room next door to her were both dying. As the social worker at this time, I always tried to be present for the patient and the family during the final few hours or minutes to offer comfort, companionship, and any help I could give.

On this evening, the nurse and I went continually back and forth from room to room, from dying woman to dying woman. It was hard to tell which one would go first. As it turned out, only one died that night.

Mrs. Helms grew weaker as her breathing changed. I sat by her bed and watched her, and in doing so realized I was also listening to her, especially to her breathing. And then I thought I heard something else. With each breath, with each inhale and exhale, it seemed she was saying, "Hen-ry . . . Hen-ry . . . Hen-ry . . ." As I paid more attention, I was convinced this was exactly what I was hearing. The nurse agreed.

Henry was not only the name of her deceased husband, but also of her beloved son. I had come to know the son quite well and had great respect for him, so I decided to phone him. I told him what was happening, and how she was breathing the name over and over. He very kindly thanked me for calling but said that he would not be coming. He had been there earlier in the day and had said good-bye to his mother.

I spoke to Mrs. Helms. "Henry, your son, is not coming. But your husband, Henry, is waiting for you." Within a minute or two, a large tear formed in the corner of her eye then rolled down her cheek. And she joined Henry.

SONG 25 –

THE GARDEN OF EDEN

Some people move to Springmoor from homes they lived in for thirty, forty, or even fifty years. Others moved from house to house, upgrading or downsizing, or by job transfer from one city to another before settling into Springmoor for the remainder of their retirement and their lives. (Many people know that IBM stands for I've Been Moved.) One man lived his entire life from birth until his move to Springmoor in the same house. One block from the North Carolina State University campus, his home then became a fraternity house. And one couple, who for the sake of the telling of their story, I will call Adam and Eve, moved from their own private Garden of Eden.

Unlike the more well-known Adam and Eve, this couple had no children. Their family was quite small: a sister, niece, and nephew. When I knew them, only their pastor and one young woman from church, who had "adopted" them, visited with regularity. The friend's name was Mandy.

Why would anyone leave the Garden of Eden to live in a retirement community? As with many people, there were health issues that brought this couple to Springmoor. Adam had dementia and moved directly into the health care facility. Eve had lung disease which made breathing a constant struggle. Often I would hear her raspy breaths coming down the hall well before she reached my office, and sometimes she would stop to rest and visit for a while before continuing on to see Adam. I loved hearing her stories.

Their having no children was not by choice but by fate. Twice Eve gave birth, only to hear the child cry and then die almost immediately. With deep sorrow and tenderness, Adam spoke compassionately for them as a couple by declaring, "We're not doing this anymore. We're not going to fill up the cemetery." So they made a good life for just the two of them. It was plain to see how adoring they were of each other.

Once, Eve needed to be hospitalized for a serious surgery. When she was back in her room from recovery, she awoke to a room filled with branches of dogwoods brought there by Adam from their property to make her feel at home and loved.

As I got to know their stories, I came to admire their devotion to each other. Adam was no longer able to converse, but Eve told me a lot about their lives, often talking about their home. One day when she was telling me about their house and their property, she said, "Why don't you drive in to see it sometime." So I did.

Off a secondary road just three or four miles from Springmoor was a dirt road. When Eve had told me where to find it, I realized I had passed there many times without noticing their narrow private road. The woods were thick and natural, and thus the road was not apparent until one was actually looking for it. I turned in and drove almost a mile before coming upon a stunning opening in the woods. There in the midst of the trees was a modest house and a pond with ducks. As I recall, it was springtime, and the dogwoods were blooming. What a beautiful place! Eve was thrilled when I told her of my visit there.

As with many people with dementia, the progression of Adam's disease was slow but steady. Eve, however, began to struggle more and more until it became necessary for her to move to the health care facility as well. Their friend Mandy came often, and I visited as much as I could.

Eve knew she was dying and was anxious, as are many patients with breathing difficulties. On my visits, we talked as much as she could tolerate, and both Mandy and I tried to offer comfort, reassurance, and love.

Then came an evening when it was apparent that Eve's life was coming to an end. The nurse phoned me, and I, in turn, phoned Mandy. We brought Adam to the room to say good-bye to his beloved wife in his limited yet knowing way. And then she was gone.

I arrived early at the cemetery for her memorial service. The gravedigger, the only person yet there, was preparing a small place for her ashes to be interred. It was my privilege to commit her ashes to the beautiful earth she and Adam so loved.

For many years now, every time I have driven down the road past their property, I think of Eve and Adam. The property has been sold, and a development with at least 150 houses has been built there. The pond is still there, glimmering in the sun behind some of the houses.

I wonder if the current residents know they are living in the Garden of Eden. Surely this Adam and Eve knew.

SONG 26 –

A LIFETIME OF LOVE

"Miss" Gladys and Mr. Ernest were there in Baltimore when I was born. Well, not actually there at the hospital. They were at home in their apartment across the hall from ours caring for my sister Barbara, who was seven years old.

The day before I was born, Barbara had gotten permission to cross the street with some other girls to a little store to buy candy. Since it was nearing Halloween, she bought some red wax lips. As they were returning home, Barbara, the last one in the group, was trying to keep up with the others and ran out in front of a car. She was carried on the front end of the car for several yards before she fell off. Both tires on one side of the car drove over both her legs. The driver did not stop. Miraculously, the only injuries Barbara had were a bad cut above the eye and massive bruising.

Mama and Gladys were sitting in the yard and heard the accident. Ernest was nearby and ran there ahead of them. When he saw the wax lips in Barbara's mouth and the blood from her forehead running down her face, he was sure she was gravely injured. Then realizing what the lips were, he threw them as hard and as far as he could. Of course, there is little question as to why I was born the next day. My poor mother.

Gladys and Ernest were unable to have children and, for some reason, were never successful in adopting a child. So they showered all their love on us. Though I don't remember it, my mother talked about how Ernest would let me drink out of his glass, my baby slobber and all, and how he would get on the floor and play with us and let us comb his hair. They adored us, and we loved them dearly.

My parents were originally from North Carolina, so it was good news and terrible news when my father got a job that would move us back to North Carolina. I have carried in my mind's eye all my life an image of Miss Gladys and Mr. Ernest standing in the yard by our car, telling us good-bye. All our hearts were breaking. It was my second birthday.

Eventually, they too left Baltimore and moved to Florida, and then back to their native West Virginia. If they were traveling north or south, they would stop and visit us. And at least once, after my father died, my mother, my sisters, and I visited them in West Virginia. Of course, there were always the highly anticipated Christmas cards and the rare telephone calls. I even made a visit on my own when I was in my mid-twenties and in West Virginia for other purposes.

As I recall, Ernest died first and then Gladys a few years later. They probably never dreamed the day I was born that now, more than six decades later, they would still be with me every day. In life, in death, in life.

SONG 27 –

THE LITTLE CHILDREN OF THE WORLD

On her eightieth birthday, Lena expressed an unusual reason for celebration. With a big sigh of relief and a tentative smile, she said, "Now I don't have to remember everything anymore." Her husband Bill, her sister Esther, and I had gathered to wish her a happy birthday and eat some cake and ice cream. It would not be her last birthday, but none of the remaining ones would be the same, for she was plunging headlong into the depths of dementia.

Though they had tried to keep this from me, I knew already. I had seen more than enough dementia in my work, and I was seeing distinct and disturbing changes in my dear friend. (When I had first fully comprehended what was happening, I had sat on my bed and read twenty-five years' worth of Lena's letters, sobbing and sobbing.) As the dementia developed, Lena complained each time she, Bill, and I gathered to visit of not being able to hear Bill. I reasoned that though her hearing might truly be somewhat diminished, the real reason was that she could not follow a three-way conversation and did not want him with us, but rather preferred our long-standing, customary tête-à-têtes. Lena would become tense and agitated which was not at all like her. Also, the two of them had become more and more reclusive. Though Bill was quiet and studious, Lena was a woman who adored people and was adored in return. In times past, when she walked, she almost skipped. Now she was reserved and insecure. This was not normal.

One afternoon when I phoned to ask if I might come visit, I received the usual warm welcome. Before my arrival, Bill and Esther prepared Lena to tell me she was losing her memory. The four of us gathered for a short time, and then Bill and Esther left us alone. When dear Lena nervously told me her memory was failing, I gently replied, "I know. But I want you to know that even if one day you don't know me, I will always love you, and I will always know you love me." She heaved a big sigh. After that, our visits were filled with the old joy we had always shared.

I had known them since I was twelve years old, and I adored Lena especially. (See Song 9) She was a spiritual mother to me, and I was the daughter she never had. Though she had great respect for my mother and never wanted to overstep any boundaries, she privately called me her "child." We did fun things together and spent countless hours talking in their formal living room. Lena played the piano and I sang while Bill watched TV in the den. She still played a few classical pieces she had learned when majoring in piano in college. When she played one particular piece, Bill always came in the room. It was "their song" from their courting days. When she cooked dinner and invited me (which was often), I did the dishes. The two of them allowed me access to their private lives not granted many.

The public version of Lena and Bill was quite well known in Baptist circles in North Carolina, other states, and around the world. They used their own funds to visit Baptist mission work in North, Central, and South America, Africa, Asia, and Europe. The purpose was to return to churches and camps in the United States to share the ways missionaries were serving. "Preaching, Teaching, and Healing" was a theme they often used in their presentations.

They had some adventures beyond their expectations, not always wanted. In Alaska when the missionaries took them out on the Arctic ice, the ice broke, and Lena fell into the frigid water. She was taken immediately to a nearby home, (as a young person, I always envisioned an igloo), stripped down, and wrapped in a fur blanket. On another occasion, while on a trip overseas, they saw a woman walking down a street wearing a lovely dress common in that culture. Since they collected clothing articles from each country, they asked their driver to stop and ask the woman where they could get one for Lena. The gracious woman invited them home with her and insisted Lena take that very dress. She also insisted that Lena try it on, so she could show her how to wear it properly. Upon returning to the mission station, they showed the garment to the missionaries and told them the story. The surprised missionaries asked where this had happened, and when they learned the location, they exclaimed, "Oh, no! A woman living in that area probably has lice!" Lena did not get lice, but said she itched for weeks just thinking of the possibility. All in the name of God's love.

On their visits to the missionaries, Lena and Bill observed a custom shared among missionary families who served together. The children in those families called the adults "Aunt" or "Uncle." And so, as I got to know Lena and Bill, they invited me to call them Aunt Lena and Uncle Bill as the missionary kids called them.

They were fortunate to make a trip to mainland China in May 1980. (In fact, they were there when Mount St. Helens erupted in Washington.) Together with a group of prominent Baptists, they visited places where missionaries had not been permitted in decades but had been of faithful service prior to communist rule.

When they traveled, Uncle Bill took thousands of photographs. One outstanding picture from the China trip showed Aunt Lena standing beside their tour bus engulfed by dozens of eager, smiling Chinese school children. The memory of that photo is fixed in my mind because I knew the attraction those children were feeling. Aunt Lena was like a magnet drawing children to her.

As Lena's dementia progressed, the time came when Bill and Esther could no longer meet her care needs, so she was moved to the nursing center adjacent to their retirement community. I visited mostly on weekends. Some of those times Bill or Esther was present. At other times, I was alone with my precious Aunt Lena.

Her physical and mental capacities deteriorated, and her language abilities failed. But since I had known her so long and so well, I could usually chatter away and maintain a connection with her.

In December before her last Christmas, I was alone in the room with Aunt Lena one afternoon when I noticed a stack of Christmas cards by her bed. Taking them in hand, I showed her the pictures, read them to her, and reminded her of all the love that was being sent to her. Then a most precious thing happened. There among the cards was a card depicting the world surrounded by children dressed in clothing representative of their various cultures and countries. "All the little children of the world." As I showed the card to Aunt Lena and talked to her about Jesus' love for all the children of the world, with quivering chin, she smiled and said, "Yes!" and a tear slipped down her cheek.

I visited with her alone for several hours the night before she died and was able, one last time, to say all that my heart held dear for her. But I was officiating a funeral when she died the next afternoon. For me, though, I will always hear "Yes!" and see the tear on her cheek when I think of all the children of the world and my lovable, loving Aunt Lena.

SONG 28 –

THE GIFT OF BEAUTY

Carol was one of the most beautiful women I have ever known. The thing is that she was beautiful in so many ways. She was very pretty, stylish but not overdone. No matter her hair style, it was always just right. Her hands and nails were perfectly manicured. When her weight fluctuated up or down by a few pounds, it was never too much, but rather was an indication of her happiness. And by anyone's guess, she looked ten or fifteen years younger than she was. She had a gentle, humble spirit but a wicked sense of humor. She was a loving, attentive daughter, sister, and wife, a fiercely faithful mother to her three daughters, a proud grandmother and great-grandmother, and a kind, true friend. Her upbringing in a Christian home and the Baptist church and her love for the Triune God created at her center a beautiful spirit.

The icing on the cake, however, was that Carol was a gifted pianist. Though the word "talented" is often used to describe one's musical abilities, in Carol's case, her music was truly a gift from God. She could read any music put in front of her but she could also hear a song for the first time on the radio in the car then walk in the house, sit down at the piano, and play it.

From the time she was a child studying piano with a woman in her church, Carol began playing piano for church services. As the years passed, she played for several gospel groups as well. In fact, she rarely said no to any opportunity to play for the worship and glory of God.

I first met Carol when I was in seminary. I was working part time at a small private business owned by a retired minister who also hosted an early Sunday morning television program on the local station. As he preached a short sermon, an interpreter for the deaf stood near him, signing. I was one of two singers on the program, and Carol was the pianist. From the beginning, I knew she was someone special.

As time passed, Carol and I performed together often. We were a perfect match since, for both of us, hymns were what we loved most. We put together hymn medleys and did programs in churches. When a hymn was pitched too high, Carol could, without much thought, lower it to another key. If one was too low, she could raise it a half step or step higher. She could modulate between keys with ease. Occasionally, she would accidentally put me in the key of "Gee-whiz!" Since she knew all the words to the hymns, she even breathed with me. In addition to those times of worship through music, we also did some secular programs which were quite fun.

Living on opposite sides of town, we did not see each other in the grocery store or at church or eating at restaurants. But any time I called her to play for me, after checking schedules, she was always ready and willing. We had wonderful times together, and even had the opportunity to record a CD.

After Carol's divorce from her first husband, the father of her three daughters, she married Jim. God was surely the matchmaker, for they were the perfect couple. Jim supported all her music activities and loved her large family, and she supported his caring of his mother and sister. He joined the church which was so dear to Carol's heart and became involved in working with the senior adults of the church. They could not have been happier.

Following the terrorist attacks on 9/11, Carol and Jim went to New York City to work as volunteers in cleaning up the area surrounding Ground Zero. They worked in nearby apartments, helping people begin to put their lives back together.

One day I was in my office when the phone rang. It was Carol. "Phyllis," she said, "I'm in the hospital and wanted you to know. I have lung cancer, and I'd like to see you." I was stunned as I made my way quickly to the car and drove the six miles to the hospital. How could my beautiful friend have lung cancer? She didn't smoke. Jim didn't smoke. I could not comprehend it.

When I arrived at her hospital room, it was apparent Carol was indeed quite ill. Diagnostic testing had been done and treatments had already begun. She was very weak. Eventually she went home. When I visited there, she and Jim and the daughters told me that laboratory testing had shown the cancer to be the kind that workers at the 9/11 site were developing. Her good work, her kind, loving heart, her caring hands had exposed her to this deadly disease. Gone was her hair. Also gone was the strength to play the piano.

By God's grace, through Carol's own determination, and with the prayers of many who loved her, she became strong enough to play again. No, not for programs such as the ones we had done together, but on a couple of occasions she was able to play at church. Slightly less than a month before she died, she had regained enough "muscle memory" to make a recording of hymn arrangements so deeply embedded in her mind and spirit. What a blessing this has been over the years.

Finally, when she was so weak and sick that even her devoted family could no longer meet all her needs, Carol was moved to the tranquil and lovely hospice home in Raleigh. I had an emotional and meaningful time there with her and Jim, with Jan and June, her twins, Terri, her youngest daughter, and with a few of her young adult grandchildren.

Carol's funeral was held in her beloved home church. Instead of the usual organ prelude to the service, the recording of hymns she had made with such love, dedication, and determination was played as the church filled to capacity. I had been invited to sing, probably at Carol's request. By God-given strength, I was able to make it through without my voice breaking, for my precious friend Carol. She was then buried in the church cemetery where many loved ones had taken their places before her.

I have had many accompanists in my life of singing. I have had many friends. But Carol was, by all measures, the most beautiful, outside and inside.

SONG 29 –

FULL CIRCLE

I got to know my friend as she was taking her first steps to recovery following a life-altering divorce. She was deeply wounded. Thankfully, she had two older teenage sons whom she adored most of the time and was tempted to throttle part of the time, for they were, after all, young, normal guys.

As the years passed, this friend, two others, and I became "a little group," going out to lunch and sometimes to movies. We shared our woes and our joys. By then, the boys were young men and away from home.

Before six o'clock one Saturday morning, my phone rang. I was sound asleep, but when I heard my friend's voice on the other end, I was jolted awake by her near hysteria. She had just received a call saying that her older son had become critically ill overnight and was, in fact, brain-dead, though still being kept alive artificially. On her way out the door for the almost three-hour drive to the hospital, she asked that I call our two other friends, and that I go see her mother in person and tell her the grim news which, at the appropriate time, we would also share with her invalid father.

On the Wednesday preceding this Saturday morning call, her son had visited his mom, brother, and grandparents. They had lunch together during this week between Christmas and New Year's Day. Everyone was well and happy.

On Friday, he called his mom to tell her he was in the hospital but believed he would be alright in a few days. He had gone through a bout of the same serious sickness a couple of years earlier and had gotten well. Later Friday night while he was in the hospital room alone, he took an overwhelming turn for the worse and was found unresponsive by a nurse. There was little hope.

Over the weekend, the other two friends and I talked several times. We decided we would make the drive out of town to the hospital on Monday, and we would offer to take the grandmother as well. She agreed to join us.

When we arrived at the hospital, the atmosphere was bleak. Family members were going in and out of the room where their loved one lay motionless. His mother invited me into the room. The sight was shocking. Not that he looked so bad, but that he looked so good. Had I not known the situation, I would have expected this handsome, fit young man to wake up, start talking, and get out of bed. But that would not happen.

A few hours later, the family was asked to gather in a small conference room. The grandmother, my friends, and I waited. When our friend, the mother, came out, she shared with us that they had made the decision to take him off life support the next day and donate organs. This they did.

I was asked to speak at the funeral. It was one of the most difficult requests I have ever had. But for my friend, I had to do it, and even more, I wanted to do it.

Over the weeks, months, and years, my friend struggled mightily. She still struggles today, truth be told, for a mother *never* "gets over" the loss of a child. Every year she takes the anniversary day of his death off work to spend alone in reflection. But she has also learned to laugh again, and to go on as life continues to throw rocks at her.

There was a woman we came to know a few years later who was caring for a family member, a young man about the same age as my friend's son. He had come from another state and had been waiting for months to receive a life-saving transplant. As his name moved near the top of the list, he was hospitalized where he continued to wait for many weeks.

A group of people, including my friend, prayed for him regularly. On the anniversary of her son's death, she decided she wanted to meet this young man, and so she visited him in the hospital since his local family had gone several states away for a much-needed vacation.

While they visited, the young man said he would like to go to the sunroom of the hospital for a brief escape from the confines of his room. My friend gladly accommodated him. They were talking when his pager went off. The look on his face told my friend everything. The organ he needed was available and on the way. He had minutes to make a final decision and get ready.

My friend's motherly instincts kicked in. Not wanting to be intrusive at such a time, she asked what she could do, thinking that perhaps he might want her to leave so he could talk to out-of-state family. But, no, he wanted her to please stay. So she did. All night. Into the next morning. Until the transplant was successfully done.

When she called me, I could hardly believe this had happened. She had now been on both ends of the life-giving miracle of organ transplantation. She knew, in full measure, what it was to give, and she witnessed what it was to receive.

Full circle.

SONG 30 –

DIFFERENT YET THE SAME

Katalin (Kati) and György were born Hungarian Jews in the 1930s. When I first knew Kathy and George beginning in 2012, they were naturalized US citizens and atheists.

Within a few months of their move to Springmoor, Kathy phoned me in the chaplain's office one day requesting a meeting with me. I had met them casually but had had little personal contact with them. Kathy had a dilemma she needed to resolve and wanted my help. As her story went, at lunch a day or two earlier, she and George were greeted by another resident who, in her Southern manner, began asking them questions about themselves including, "Where do you go to church?" When they simply replied, "We don't," the lady gasped and blurted, "Oh! I'm sorry!" This reaction flummoxed Kathy, and she wanted my thoughts on how to deal with this woman in the future and with other Christians as well here in the Bible Belt. She did not want to hurt anyone. Neither did she want to be untruthful about her atheism. Apparently, what I said rang true with Kathy, for she was not only satisfied with our conversation but decided that she "really, really" wanted to be my friend. Thus our friendship began.

Kathy invited me to use George's season ticket to attend North Carolina Symphony concerts with her. She and George invited me and another friend to their home several times for coffee. Occasionally, I had lunch with them in the Springmoor Dining Room. A few times I took them out for pizza. Most significantly, however, Kathy became a regular member of a discussion group I facilitated. The group was small enough that everyone in attendance could safely express our true feelings and views about various matters including the "no-no's," religion and politics. Kathy grew close to and trusting of the group as we all shared honestly and with true acceptance of each other. When she and George occasionally traveled for a month or more at a time, we always missed her.

On the last trip they took, George got sick and had to be cared for in the ship's infirmary. This was quite taxing for Kathy, and she confided to me that she thought their traveling days were over. This was a major change in their lives as they had made two or sometimes three major trips every year for many years. Upon their return from each trip, Kathy used her still photographs and George's videos to make beautiful travel programs complete with her narration and carefully selected classical music. These were shown in the Springmoor Auditorium, and there was an enthusiastic group of people who attended each time. The end of their travels was a significant loss for them.

One day Kathy invited me to their home for a conversation. They shared with me the news that George had been diagnosed with metastatic cancer. There would be treatment, but ultimately it was not successful. Kathy waited on him hand and foot, eager to meet his every need.

Almost simultaneous to this, Kathy began losing weight. After some weeks, she became concerned, but everyone else, including and especially me, attributed this to the strain of caring for George who was not always an easy person to be with. Finally, Mary, Kathy's friend from out of state, emailed me with Kathy's permission, forwarding the email Kathy had written to her expressing her frustrations at not being heard. By then, she was also seeing medical people who were finding nothing significant.

On Kathy's birthday, a Sunday in mid-February, I took her to lunch at one of her favorite restaurants. George chose not to go with us and was, in fact, probably too weak to go. I ordered a nice meal and expected Kathy to do the same for her birthday, but instead she chose only soup. As we talked and she told me about her frustrations with George and with her own self-perceived illness, she stuck her leg out from under the table into the aisle for me to see. When she pulled up her pant leg, I was stunned to see her grossly swollen ankle. I insisted that she make plans to go to the clinic to be seen by the doctor the very next morning. She agreed.

The next morning, I was in my office when the nurse called from the clinic saying that Kathy was being sent to the hospital emergency room. I scurried to the clinic to see Kathy then followed the ambulance to the hospital. Within a period of just a couple of hours, Kathy was diagnosed with an aggressive cancer. A few days later, I accompanied her to an appointment with an oncologist who confirmed the diagnosis and gave her two choices: (1) "try" chemotherapy or (2) call hospice. Kathy, without hesitation, said, "I'll call hospice." On the way back home, she wanted to eat at her favorite Japanese restaurant and, again, she chose soup. I suspect now that as we sat and talked that day, I was more stunned than she was. I think she had known for quite a while the seriousness of her condition.

The following week, I joined the two of them in their home when the hospice intake nurse came for a visit, and both George and Kathy signed up for hospice care. I visited as often as I could, but since they were private people, I tried hard to be supportive but not intrusive. They gave me every indication that my attention and love were helpful. In fact, Kathy seemed very needy of our opportunities to talk together.

In March, less than a month later, both of them had become weak enough that they made the decision to move out of their Springmoor house and into the Springmoor health care center. Kathy planned everything meticulously, including how to get both their beds, their two chairs and ottomans, an occasional table, and one large computer in the room. She even set up a makeshift kitchen. Since they had no family in the United States, a team of staff members joined forces to empty their house. While this was gut-wrenching for the staff, knowing that we were disposing of their treasures collected over a lifetime, Kathy and George walked out the door and never looked back. Their final journey had begun.

For a while, George enjoyed ordering food from various restaurants, including the Japanese restaurant, and having it delivered. It was almost like a game for him. But Kathy's appetite continued to wane. She grew thinner and thinner, eating soup and soup alone. She was beginning to have the appearance of a Holocaust victim, the very thing she had survived as a child.

Most days Kathy seemed very much to enjoy my company, and George managed to tolerate me. When she felt like it, Kathy and I would walk a short distance down the hall to a small room where we could talk privately. We talked about many subjects, including the depth of our unusual friendship, their future days, their deaths, and religion. From the beginning of our friendship, we had been open about my Christianity and her atheism. But one day during this period as she marched toward death Kathy said, "I sometimes envy your faith."

My heart ached for Kathy. I believed then, and still do, that I was the only person physically present in her life in whom she could confide deeply about her fears, disappointments, frustrations, and desires. And this she did with caution. George and Kathy had each suffered great loss in Hungary during the Holocaust, and both had learned then to keep a lid on their feelings, especially George. When George's temper flared or Kathy grew frustrated with people treating other people without regard for their humanity, I had only a smidgen of understanding of what they must have witnessed and experienced. (Kathy's friend Mary, her "glue," called occasionally, but any phone conversations they could have were always in the presence of George, and Kathy did not always feel free to talk openly. They did, however, communicate for a while by email, which was somewhat satisfying to them both.)

One day in April, I went to their room to visit. Kathy wanted to go down the hall to talk. When we got seated in the tiny room, she exploded in anger. According to her, I did not know the meaning of personal space, and I had invaded hers. I was deeply hurt by this, and our conversation did not go well, I regret to say. I soon left, in tears by the time I walked with her back to her room. I went for a five-hour drive to get my emotions back under control. For a couple of days, I allowed some space between Kathy and me until Kathy called and asked me to please come back. We were able to talk through what had happened and to forgive each other. For this, we were both very thankful. I had learned a hard and painful lesson. But we succeeded in letting go of any hurt as her needs rapidly increased. In fact, our bond grew stronger, we agreed, because, as trusted friends, we had been brave enough to be honest with each other.

As May passed into June, Kathy continued growing weaker. She had a lovely private attendant much of the time yet still insisted on getting dressed and out of bed every day until late June. By then, she was no longer able to sit up in a chair and was taking almost no nourishment. George was, ironically, not changing as fast as Kathy, though he had been diagnosed much longer. He occupied much of his time using his personal tablet as Kathy was fading away.

One evening at the end of June, I was in their room where I had been all day. It was apparent that Kathy had only hours to live. Even then she was dressed in her slacks and blouse, willfully doing it her way. She was restless and obviously uncomfortable. A gentle and lovely new private attendant was there that evening. I sat for a long time at Kathy's bedside, and the attendant sat at the end of the bed. I talked quietly to Kathy, assuring her that we would be with her. Finally, I got up and whispered in her ear, "Why don't you let us put a hospital gown on you and let the nurse give you some morphine." She nodded in agreement.

After that, we waited. Kathy grew calm and peaceful. George could not watch the leave-taking of the only person he loved and allowed in his wounded heart. But he did get up and speak tenderly to her when I encouraged him to do so. The attendant and I were privileged to be present to her as she was slipping away. I held her hand and told her to go to her mother, who had died when Kathy was five years old. And so she did.

George was quietly inconsolable. He lost the love of his life and, together with her, his will to live. Then he too stopped eating. He died in September.

A few friends and I scattered a portion of their ashes in the Springmoor memorial garden and later placed the remainder of their ashes in the Atlantic Ocean.

I tell this story because I feel so blessed to have had Kathy and George as my friends. They were as different in background and belief from me as possible. Yet I learned that even across great divides, people can know and care for, and, yes, love each other. They will forever be in my heart and in my dreams. Based on their beliefs, I will not see them again. But in my spirit, I believe I will. And we shall be the same.

SONG 31 –

THE MAKINGS OF A FINE MAN

Kindness, contentment, and charity are good foundations for a fine man. Bill was such a man. With his plaid shirts, high-waisted, pressed jeans, athletic shoes, and ever-present smile, he looked the part of a happily retired gentleman with nothing to prove. Even and especially with the death of his beloved wife, his faith was strong, and he found solace and joy in regular interaction with friends. And since he never met a stranger, he had a lot of friends.

Bill was a man of high principles. Grounded in his faith, he was no pushover when it came to questions of integrity. He had a strong sense of right and wrong and was not afraid to let his opinions be known, yet in the most gracious of ways.

Most people alive would consider themselves rich beyond their dreams to be loved by their families as Bill was loved by his small family: a daughter, son-in-law, grandson, nephews, and a niece. They could not help but adore a man who cherished them so much.

One day I encountered Bill sitting in one of the common areas at Springmoor, chatting with a group of friends. I mentioned to this group in passing that I was going the next week on vacation to the beach. A few minutes later, when I was back in my office, Bill appeared at the door. "I want you to cancel your reservations and go to my condo at the beach." I thanked him but explained that I really could not do that. But he was insistent, so I gratefully accepted. That was not the last time he came to my door to offer charity.

Each fall, Bill would call and ask if he could come visit me in my office. I saw him almost daily on campus and nearly every Sunday evening at our Vespers service. But on these fall visits, he came making an offering. "I have money that needs to be given away by the end of the year. What do you suggest?" he would ask. The first time I had to think a bit, but then I realized that the Springmoor community would be hosting a food packaging event in the late winter for a locally founded international organization called STOP HUNGER NOW (later renamed RISE AGAINST HUNGER). Before the end of the year, a large check from Bill was in my hands. Though he gave to other charities as well, this became a favorite for him in the years to follow.

Then one fall when he came, we had not planned the usual food packaging event. This time Bill rephrased his question to "What do we need?" I took a big leap and said, "A new grand piano for the Auditorium". He agreed to pay half if Springmoor would pay the other half. Done. Though the gift was anonymous, I furtively eyeballed him each time it was played. No one enjoyed it more than Bill.

A couple of years later on a Sunday evening, a woman motioned for me to come over to her before Vespers began so she could ask me a question. "Why can't we get some chairs for the Auditorium that are more comfortable than these?" The next morning Bill was once again in my office, this time offering to buy the chairs. It was only several years later, at his memorial service, that I was finally given permission by his daughter to tell about Bill's generous gifts of the piano and chairs.

It was a joy to celebrate Bill's ninetieth birthday with him, his family, and a few friends. No one would have guessed he was that age. But as the next few years went by, there were some subtle hints that things were changing. He gradually lost weight and sometimes was not quite as sharp as he had been, but there was nothing in particular to be alarmed about.

Then Bill got sick and had to be hospitalized. When he was discharged, he went home to his beloved house at Springmoor where his daughter, son-in-law, namesake grandson William, niece, and an employed caregiver ministered to his needs with the support of a visiting hospice team.

When I called to ask if I might come for a visit, the daughter most graciously welcomed me. Seeing Bill confined to his bed shook me. But his gentleness, kindness, and joy were very much the same. Though weak, he greeted me with such warmth and thanked me for coming. I knew he was not able to endure a long visit, so I offered a prayer together with my thanks and appreciation for his treasured friendship to me and to so many and, giving him a little kiss on the check, told him I loved him. He replied with a smile and much enthusiasm, "I love people!"

Yes Bill, you too were much loved and will always be missed. But I know there is a wife who was happy to greet you when you joined her in the place God had prepared for you. A place complete with beautiful music and comfortable chairs, where there are no hungry children.

SONG 32 –

THE STRENGTH OF LOVE

"Opposites attract." This familiar adage is borne out in the marriage story of Moppy and Chuck. Or as their daughter Charlotte refers to them: always "Mother," and usually "Daddy," sometimes "Chuck-Ol'Boy."

After their move to an apartment in South Village at Springmoor, it took Chuck no more than a week to secure a spot in a nice wing-back chair near the entrance and security desk where he sat daily for hours, greeting anyone and everyone who passed by. In short order, he knew everyone and their grandmother if they still had one. People soon affectionately began calling him the mayor of South Village.

While Moppy knew how to be social and enjoyed parties and dancing, she was not by nature ebullient like Chuck. She preferred quieter activities in their apartment.

If someone said they needed something from the grocery store, Chuck was in his car in the blink of an eye to shop for them. If someone needed a ride back from the car repair shop, where Chuck had gotten to know the owner personally, he was ready to give them a lift. Moppy gifted friends with needlepoint bookmarks.

Chuck was well-groomed but carried some extra weight. Moppy looked, dressed, and carried herself proudly like a model.

Moppy's claims to fame were two: one of her exquisite needlepoint pieces was part of the décor at Blair House in Washington, DC; she was introduced to Princess Grace of Monaco just days before the tragic death of the princess. Moppy deeply mourned that death.

Chuck's claim to fame was that his mother lived to the ripe old age of 107.

Chuck indulged their daughter with any and everything she might want. Moppy, on the other hand, was always hard on Charlotte. A bit jealous, I suspect, of the relationship between father and daughter, she, nevertheless, craved Charlotte's attention and love. But she never eased up on Charlotte about losing weight, though Charlotte was always as stylishly dressed and groomed as her mother. As I became friends with them, she included my own need to slim down in that conversation as well. I took it as a sign of her affection and trust in our friendship. But I must admit, it would have been hard had I been hearing it all my life.

One of the best things that ever happened to that small family was Charlotte's marriage to Oliver. Charlotte married a little later than some young women, and Oliver's age was somewhere in the middle between her age and the age of her parents. Calm, easy-going, patient, yet willing to speak up when necessary, he was the ballast for the family when they listed to one side or the other.

Moppy, Chuck, and I attended the same church. From my vantage point in the choir, I saw Moppy on the back row most Sundays, and sometimes Chuck.

One day Chuck called, asking me to come visit in their apartment. He felt the desire to be baptized but, because of his physical size and age, he did not want to be immersed. We talked with the church's pastor, and with the bending of some Baptist rules, he was baptized "otherwise." He was at church almost every Sunday after that.

A few years later, Chuck got sick and needed to be admitted to the health care facility on campus. With sunlight streaming in the window, Chuck died as Moppy, Charlotte, Oliver, and I were at his side.

All of them grieved, but Chuck's death was especially hard for Moppy. A brittle diabetic, she neglected the self-care duties that come with that disease. A few times she came near the precipice of death.

Then the young children of the church came to visit on Valentine's Day.

Bearing small handmade gifts, the children visited all the members of the church who were Springmoor residents. Nothing was expensive. Nothing compared to the beauty of the needlepoint pieces Moppy created. Yet tucked into the gift was something priceless. Printed on a small piece of paper were the words from I Corinthians 13, "Love is patient and kind, does not envy, is not proud . . ."

After that visit, several weeks had passed when Moppy came to see me. She was gripped, possessed, her heart set ablaze by those words of Scripture. Night after night, day after day she had carefully meditated on the words . . . love, kindness, gentleness, and all the others, taking each word one at a time, to grasp the depth and meaning, to commit each one to memory and heart before moving on to the next. She was transformed.

She brought with her on that visit to me a carefully laid out copy of those treasured words, done as she would have for a work of needlepoint. She asked if I could print on my computer a version of what she had sketched and make it into a bookmark. I could and did. When it was designed and approved by Moppy, I printed and laminated each one. When those had been given to her friends, I made more. When those gave out, I made more.

Moppy's friends and family celebrated her ninetieth birthday with a party. There is, in my bedroom, a small photograph of us on that happy occasion as well as a treasured piece of her needlepoint work.

God's love and its place in her life changed Moppy. Yes, she was still hard on Charlotte and did not let either of us forget that we needed to lose weight. But she was softer now.

I was with her, Charlotte, and Oliver when she died. Precious wife, mother, friend.

When Moppy arrived in heaven, she was, I imagine, first greeted by Chuck sitting in a wingback chair near Saint Peter's gate. Then she was enfolded in the arms of LOVE, the God she had come to know quite well.

SONG 33 –

THE CAT'S MEOW

Born in 1908, Grace was, I am fairly certain, the cat's meow during the Roaring Twenties. With her golden blond hair, handsome good looks, and Southern charms, she surrounded herself with fun, daring friends. Some of those things never changed.

In her old age, Grace enjoyed regaling her friends with what sounded like embellished stories of traveling to Europe as a young woman with a girlfriend where they flirted with all the good-looking young men. I guess, by the time she was telling us the stories, only she knew the whole truth so who were we to dispute her!

But life was not all fun and games. Grace was a smart, hard worker. She worked in North Carolina for Governor Kerr Scott, then went to Washington to work for him when he was elected to the US Senate. Back in North Carolina, she later worked for Governor Robert Scott. They remained friends for the rest of their lives.

Grace first married Johnny. She loved him dearly and lost him too young. She continued a close relationship with her sister-in-law well into her late nineties until they were no longer able to visit or communicate.

After Johnny's death, Grace married Allen. Grace was Baptist, a liberal one, and Allen was Jewish. It worked beautifully for them. They met at Arthur Murray Studios, dancing. And they danced as long as their legs would carry them. After Allen was living in the health care center at Springmoor, he would get behind his wheelchair and dance with Grace when she visited. What a love they had.

Grace lived fifteen years after Allen died. She had a two-bedroom apartment, and it was filled to the brim. Her first task when someone visited was to clear a space for the visitor to sit. Once, she needed me to go with her to her storage bin. It was like walking into a Dr. Seuss picture. Big box on little box on square box on round box on bigger box on tiny box. All teetering precariously. She obviously never disposed of anything.

Grace loved cats. Many years earlier when she was traveling, her cat got out of the car and was lost. A few hundred miles and a couple of years later, the cat appeared at her back door. The story was featured in *Life* magazine.

She had no live cats at Springmoor but discovered she could get almost-life-like cats that purred. One, then another, then another until her bed was filled with them together with a large stuffed gorilla. By this time, she was living in a private room in the health care center, and there was simply too much stuff for her safety or that of other residents.

The social workers, the nurses, her friends, and the chaplain (me) talked to her about giving up some things. "NO!" she said. And the more we said, the more she dug in her heels. Finally, she got fed up with us and said she would "just move!" She had been at Springmoor twenty-five years, and we all thought she was bluffing. But indeed, she was not. All of us, including her long-time friends, refused to help her, thinking that would be the end of this "nonsense." Somehow, though, she sweet-talked some of the staff into bringing her some boxes. She packed and arranged her move to an assisted living facility a few blocks away. All this at age 103!

A couple of months after the move, Grace was hospitalized with a heart condition which periodically flared up. Upon discharge, Grace could not return to the facility she had moved to, so she threw in the towel and called to see if she could come back to Springmoor. She was welcomed with open arms and many smiles.

Grace was mad all day on her 105th birthday. She had planned to die on her birthday, and it was just not happening. Surrounded by friends, flowers, cake, and cards. Mad.

Several months later, she was scooting around in her motorized chair on the second floor of the health care center where she lived. She went over to the door of the physical therapy department to speak to the workers there and fell out of the chair face first on the floor. Dead.

I cannot think of any better way for Grace to have died. Though she was not walking, she was still dancing in her heart. She danced right into heaven that day, joining Johnny and Allen.

"And hand in hand, on the edge of the sand,
they danced by the light of the moon."

-From *THE OWL AND THE PUSSYCAT* by Edward Lear

SONG 34 –

A LIFE OF THANKSGIVING

Suzanne was, in a word I learned growing up in Eastern North Carolina, a "character." If you know what a "character" is, other than someone in a book or movie, then you understand. If not, I'll try to explain. Since Suzanne, too, grew up in that general part of the state, she knew quite well who and what she was.

Suzanne was funny. She could take any piece of paper and read it aloud and make people laugh. Her Southern drawl was wide enough to drive a slow tractor through, and she took good advantage of it.

Suzanne appeared prim and proper. She dressed conservatively yet stylishly, and every hair was always in place. She had a bum knee, but other than that, she was healthy well into her nineties.

Suzanne called everyone "my dear" and backed it up with a big smile and twinkling eyes. Who could not love that?

And Suzanne made everyone *feel* dear to her.

Suzanne was as faithful as any churchwoman could be. She was always there at Sunday school and church, always active, always interested, always caring, always worshiping. She was filled with gratitude. Neither did she mind sharing her opinions.

If you were Suzanne's friend, and she had plenty of them, you had a friend for life.

Suzanne had been married, but her husband died long before I knew her. They had lived most of their married life in Los Alamos, New Mexico, where, I always suspected, he worked on the Manhattan Project. That was one thing, however, that she never revealed, if indeed it was true.

Suzanne loved the people of New Mexico, especially the Native American women. She treasured the beautiful work they did with their hands, but she treasured their hearts far, far more.

I greatly valued Suzanne's support of me in my role as chaplain at Springmoor. She gave me strength by her excellent example of faithful living, and she regularly voiced her satisfaction with my work. I was, indeed, happy to have her friendship and love and offer mine in return.

Other than the painful knee she nursed for years, she was well until she wasn't anymore. And when she got sick, she did not live long.

The dear memory of Suzanne's dying days is summed up in three words: "Thank you kindly." As she lay dying, as many people came to her room to see her one last time, her words over and over and over again were "Thank you kindly. Thank you kindly. Thank you kindly." Southern drawl intact.

God must love a character, for he surely made Suzanne and filled her heart with love and thanksgiving.

Thank you kindly, Suzanne, for making us laugh, for loving us, for sharing your heart. You were a character.

SONG 35 –

SURE THING

Beulah and John moved to Springmoor in 1988. Among the younger couples, they were quite vigorous and ready to be involved in the life of their new community. They were the kind of people who were going to make contributions wherever they were, and so they quickly got busy. Within a year or two, John was elected president of the Residents' Association. Beulah continued teaching private piano lessons, but her real love was playing for worship services. She had been the organist for worship services for dozens of churches of all denominations over her lifetime. In addition, a Sunday school class at their church in Raleigh was named for John, the class's first teacher, and Beulah played piano regularly for that class.

Beulah's father was a Methodist minister. One Sunday when Beulah was nine years old, her mother, the church organist, was sick requiring her to stay at home. Beulah was called upon by her parents to play for the morning worship service. "Daddy," said she, "I am not sure if I know how to do this." He replied, "You have seen your mother do it. Just pump the big pedals on the organ, and you can do it. What hymns do you know?" She told him, he altered his sermon to fit with those hymns, and that is what they sang on her first Sunday as a church organist.

One thing that greatly concerned Beulah when they moved to Springmoor was the absence of any spiritual leadership or programming. She recruited two retired pastors to come visit people in the health care center and in the hospitals. This worked well but she was far from satisfied. When a retired Methodist minister moved to Springmoor, she worked together with him to begin Sunday evening Vespers services. Again, that was not enough. Soon they began a campaign for a chaplain. Finally, in 1992, I was given the opportunity to step into that role. What a tremendous gift Beulah brought about for me. And it was not the last by far.

Working with Beulah was an absolute joy. She was an excellent pianist. She rarely made even the slightest mistake. In fact, so few were her small mistakes that they always caught me by surprise. I have never known anyone else who was so precise. Because of her many years of playing, she knew most hymns. If they were older ones, she knew them. If they were new, she could sight read them with little effort. In addition, she was an excellent accompanist if I or anyone else was singing a solo or if she was playing for her daughter, an accomplished flutist.

Soon after Vespers was established as a regular Sunday event, Beulah decided a choir was needed. She called many friends in search of a choir director and finally found one who was faithful to the choir for fifteen years. Then, when that director retired, Beulah searched once again, successfully recruiting another dedicated and capable director. The Chapel Choir brought much joy to those who sang and added tremendously to worship. Beulah, the choir's founder and accompanist, was affectionately named "mother" of the choir.

From the time I became chaplain, Beulah and I worked together every Sunday evening with few exceptions. She also played piano for almost every memorial service held in the Springmoor Auditorium. Figuring how many services that might have been over a period of twenty-eight years, I calculate a minimum of twenty-five hundred services we did jointly. In reality, the numbers are probably far higher.

Over the years, Beulah and I became good friends. John died suddenly in 1997 while I was on a trip to the Holy Land. Beulah often stated how much she regretted my absence at that time but did allow that she was glad I was on that particular journey. She had been there several times and had experienced how holy, indeed, it was.

The one thing, however, that stands out most in my mind about Beulah was her response any time I called and asked her to play for a service not already on the schedule, mostly memorial services. Though two, maybe three times in all those years, she had no choice but to say "no," she invariably and gladly responded, "Sure thing." Countless times she cancelled other engagements or otherwise altered her personal schedule to be available.

Beulah played for Vespers the first Sunday in June 2016. A few days later, she was not feeling well and was admitted to the health care center for what we thought would be a short stay. I was privileged to be with her and her daughter when she died on June 15, fifteen days shy of her ninety-ninth birthday.

If ever there was a sure thing in my life and in the life of Springmoor, it was Beulah. And if there was a need for music when she got to heaven, I am sure she quickly and painstakingly got things organized.

Thank you, Beulah, for sharing yourself and your beautiful gift so freely.

SONG 36 –
LILY-OF-THE-VALLEY

There was a tenderness about Elizabeth that is hard to describe. Oh, in the right company, she did not mind at all expressing her opinions, strong or otherwise. She was neither shy nor retiring. Yet underlying, there was a kindness and gentleness about her that was alluring. Perhaps it was that she and Ernst, her husband of more than sixty years, always held hands when they walked together. Or maybe it was her big, cheerful smile or her carefully styled white hair. Or maybe it was the fact that she and Ernst allowed her mother to live with them for thirty-six years after the death of Elizabeth's father. I'm not sure why, but I do know that we became dear friends for reasons I cannot exactly put my finger on.

Elizabeth was born in Brooklyn to German parents, and Ernst emigrated from Germany in his early twenties. They met at a dance and were smitten with each other. When someone at that first dance casually called her Liz, she offered a stern correction, "My name is Elizabeth!" Elizabeth it was.

Her parents quickly came to appreciate Ernst and encouraged the relationship, especially with her mother's German home cooking and generous hospitality. E&E, as I liked to call them, fell in love and married. They had one son, Stefan, whom they adored.

After their move to Springmoor, as they were on the cusp of their eighties, they soon began attending Vespers services every Sunday evening, always sitting in the same place. This was in addition to their faithful attendance at their Lutheran congregation on Sunday mornings. Elizabeth also joined a conversation group that I convened twice a month. Most of the time she preferred to listen, but when she spoke everyone else listened. She thought carefully about what she said, and she was worth hearing. The odd thing was that she talked with her eyes closed. She knew she did this, and when I got to know her well enough to ask why, she could not explain it except to say that she thought more clearly that way. She was usually one of the last people to leave that group, and each time she was sure to give me a special hug which I gladly received and returned.

Over time, I grew quite fond of Elizabeth and Ernst, but I must give Elizabeth credit for making our friendship. She loved cake, but Ernst ate no sweets at all. So when she had cake, she brought me cake. She loved flowers too. One day she called and asked if I would be in my apartment for the next few minutes. The two of them soon came to my door, bearing a bouquet of lily-of-the-valley. It was raining at the time, and the weather was growing cooler at night. Ernst had stood in the yard and held the umbrella over Elizabeth while she cut the flowers. I don't know if the flowers or the act of cutting them in the rain was sweeter.

I ate dinner with them once every few weeks, and we always laughed so loudly that others looked at us as though they too wished to be having so much fun. Ernst is one of the best story tellers I know, and all the stories are funny. Of course, Elizabeth listened and laughed as though she had never heard them before. She also enjoyed watching me laugh as the love of her life entertained. They also talked affectionately about Stefan and daughter-in-law, Chris, who lived out of state.

An unusual thing about Elizabeth that was almost unspoken was her sense of her own mortality. That is not something most people dwell on, or, if they do, are unwilling to speak of. But Elizabeth did. She was not morose. She just simply had an awareness that she would not live for a long, long time. In her last years, she had an ever-growing sense that something was not right in her body. She suffered a minor stroke that, for a time, made her weak and slowed her walking, but she recovered. Nevertheless, the thought of dying was always in the back of her mind. I was glad she could share this with Ernst and me.

Early in 2019, my aunt died at age 103, but I was unable to attend her service in Florida. My cousin, her only daughter, came to North Carolina for a family reunion in October. She arrived at the airport on a Saturday, and we drove to the beach. My sisters, a niece and her children, and a nephew came that day, and a dozen or so local cousins were expected for a big lunch the next day. In addition, my cousin and I had planned a small memorial for my aunt.

When I awoke on Sunday morning, I checked the email on my phone to see if there were any messages from work. Right away I saw Elizabeth's name. She had suffered a massive stroke in the night and was in the intensive care unit at a Raleigh hospital three hours away from where I presently was. I was miserable all day Sunday yet, somehow, I enjoyed the precious time with my family. That evening as Elizabeth's condition bore on my mind, I told my cousin and my sisters that I felt a strong need to go back to Raleigh for the day on

Monday to see Elizabeth. If she died and I did not at least make an attempt to see her, I would not be able to forgive myself.

I arrived at the hospital about noon on Monday. Ernst was there alone with Elizabeth, and it was obvious that the stroke was devastating. The doctor soon came in, and it was agreed that per Elizabeth's wishes and instructions there would be no heroic efforts to save her life. Stefan and Chris were on the way, and the goal was for her to live long enough for them to say good-bye.

I drove back to the beach that evening with a heavy heart. My cousin and I had planned to stay until Friday, but as the week passed and I kept tabs on Elizabeth, I decided that we would need to come back home on Thursday. By the time I arrived, Elizabeth had been discharged from the hospital to the health care center in the Springmoor community. Ernst, Stefan, and Chris had settled in with her to care for her in her last days.

Elizabeth died the following Tuesday as Ernst stood by her bed singing in German, "Auf Wiedersehen," a love song of farewell. Stefan, Chris, and I had the privilege of being there with her as well. There were many tears. Tears of joy at having known and loved her. Tears of thanksgiving at knowing she was now with God. Tears of sorrow at her absence and at the days and years to come without her.

At Christmas, I gave a small red glass heart to Ernst, and one to Stefan and Chris. Ernst carries it in his shirt pocket always. At bedtime, as he says "good night" to Elizabeth, he places the heart on the bedside table nested in his wedding ring, then reaches out beside him for her hand. She is there, Ernst. She will always be with you.

SONG 37 –
POTATOES AND PENCILS

Using the superlative when describing something is, at best, a blessing. Using the superlative, at worst, is a poor habit. It is tempting to say, "That is the best apple pie I ever tasted," or "It was the worst movie I've ever seen." Best time of my life. Easiest test I ever took. Most evil person to ever walk the face of the earth. Greatest player to ever play the game. Scariest experience you can imagine. The worst cold anyone has ever had. The deepest snow or the hottest day. The saddest story or the funniest joke. Yes, using the superlative is often the easiest out!

Referring to food, books, games, or weather is one thing. Using the superlative to speak of people is another. It is, in fact, risky. But I can say without hesitation that Hannah was the best friend I ever had. There is no describing this friendship in any other way. It is simply the truth.

There is a temptation at this point to tell too much. In reality, I cannot record everything about Hannah as I remember and feel it. It would be the book of seventeen years of my life. So instead, I will share two stories with you. One is Hannah's own story. Then I will tell mine.

Hannah's story as taken from her memoirs, A GOOD LIFE, written in 2005:

Early in life, the church had a large part in my life. My parents attended the nearby Baptist church, and the children went with them. It was a rural church with preaching services two Sundays a month. Our church shared the preacher with another church in the area. We had Sunday school every Sunday. Revival services were held each summer, and special efforts were made to have in attendance all in the community who were not church members, hoping non-Christians would accept Christ and unite with the church.

One summer night, I went with my parents to a nearby church to hear a beloved former pastor preach the revival. The sermon that night was on the Cross – how Christ, the Son of God, was crucified for the sins of people. The preacher said Christ loved all people and he died on the Cross for all people. He said any who confessed their sins and disobedience and believed in Christ as Savior from sin would be saved. (John 3:16)

In the service that night I was very much aware of my sins, disobedience, wrongdoing, and wanted to be forgiven. When the invitation hymn was sung, I asked God to forgive me, and I felt that He did. I felt loved and happy. However, I did not go forward in the service to let my decision be known, which is customary in Baptist churches. I confused becoming a Christian with joining the church. The church in which we were meeting was not my church, and I felt that going forward in the service meant that I would like to unite with that church. I did not want to do that. It was not "my" church.

Later, in my home church in a worship service, I did go forward at the conclusion of the worship service, acknowledging my acceptance of Christ as Savior. Within a few weeks, I was baptized in the river near our church since, at that time, the church did not have an inside baptismal pool.

At times, Christians may doubt their salvation experience. I never do because of an experience I had the morning after I was baptized.

As a child, I had some chores I did in keeping with my age and abilities. One chore was scraping the skins from new potatoes that had been dug from the garden. The skin in the eyes of the potatoes was not easy to remove, and I did not always do a good job. Sometimes my mother would ask me to do some potatoes over. At times, she may have just redone my work without asking me to do it. Mothers are like that, you know.

The morning after I was baptized, I had a distinct feeling that I wanted to do a good job of scraping the potatoes – I was a Christian, a new person in Christ. A change had occurred in my life. I worked hard on the potatoes. When I returned the potatoes to Mother, she examined them carefully, hugged me to her, and said, "Hannah, you have done a good job on the potatoes this morning. Thank you."

I think Mother had seen changes in me and wanted to encourage me as a Christian. Her words and hug that morning have meant much to me and have helped me always try to do good work.

People watch us. They notice what we do. They hear what we say. When we become a Christian, our actions, our words, our attitudes need to reflect Christ in our lives.

Now, my story of Hannah:

Hannah preferred to write with pencils. Unless she was writing a formal letter using a pen or typewriter, she used a short pencil, often no more than two or three inches long. She had them in her apartment at the ready. She always had one in her purse. Since I rarely write with a pencil, I was fascinated by this. "Why do you write with a pencil? The writing smears," I teased her. "So I can erase my mistakes or make changes," she so logically replied.

She wrote down the title of every book she read, every movie we watched. Agendas, committee meeting notes, attendance lists, and lists of every sort.

When we went on trips in my car, as soon as our seat belts were fastened and the car was in reverse, she pulled a small spiral notebook from her purse with accompanying pencil. "What are you writing?" I would inquire, already knowing the answer. "I am writing down what time we're leaving so I can answer that question when you ask me later today. And by the way, what is the mileage on the car? You'll want to know that too." She wrote down the times we made rest stops, when we stopped to eat, and what we ate. She also recorded every penny she spent and would have recorded mine too if I had asked.

Hannah made written records of our trips to Lancaster County and Gettysburg, Pennsylvania, and to Washington, DC. I took pictures.

She took notes. When we traveled to the mountains or beaches in North Carolina, all activities and expenses were duly recorded. The same goes for our trips to South Carolina and Alabama to visit her former co-workers and friends. The one time she did not write on the spot was when we heard President Jimmy Carter teach Sunday school in Plains, Georgia. She wept instead, overwhelmed with awe.

In 2001, we had made all arrangements for a trip to New Mexico beginning September 19. After the terrorist attacks in the United States and the ensuing chaos of travel, we cancelled our plans. We continued to talk about it but laid aside those plans when we decided to take a cruise to Alaska in 2005. You guessed it. Hannah kept a thorough diary of all our adventures in that other-worldly state.

When 2006 came, I began to think about the postponed trip to New Mexico that Hannah had so much wanted to take. Since she was in her mid-eighties and had had multiple back and hip surgeries, I knew it was now or never. We talked at length and then decided to schedule the trip once again, inviting my sisters, Barbara and Teresa, to go with us. What a wonderful time we had staying at Glorieta Baptist Conference Center, exploring much of New Mexico, and laughing until we hurt. Precious memories. All these and more were recorded in Hannah's daily diaries as well. In pencil.

Within the first few months of Hannah's move to Springmoor in January 1988, she realized a need for worship opportunities in the health care center. She spoke with me and also with the director of activities. We both strongly supported the idea. Hannah enlisted a small group of women to serve as conveners on a rotating basis, with herself in the lead. In addition, she recruited three or four people who would play piano. And finally, she compiled an impressive list of ministers who would be invited periodically to give a short sermon during the thirty-minute Vespers services.

Hannah was fully invested in this service opportunity. For many years, she was always at the health center Vespers at four o'clock on Sunday afternoons unless she was out of town or not well. There came a time when she had a surgery, requiring others to take the lead for Vespers, but there was no doubt who was still in charge.

On Thanksgiving Day 2007, she had lunch with me at my home. After eating, we watched a dog show on television, and in the late afternoon, we both fell asleep in our chairs in the living room. About 6:30 pm, she called my name to wake me. She was very ill.

I drove Hannah to the emergency room and, from there, she was admitted to the hospital. Ultimately, we learned she had developed a serious heart condition. Although it was difficult to comprehend, we were also told that nothing could be done to help her except using oxygen and waiting.

Upon discharge from the hospital, she was admitted to the health care center at Springmoor. Ironically, it was late Sunday afternoon. Time for the Vespers service.

Hannah tried as hard as anyone I have ever seen, but she could not get better. Even in the midst of her ever-changing condition, she was the same serene person I had come to deeply love and admire. Over the next ten days, she was alert but grew weaker and weaker. I was with her every day, as much as possible. Still she made lists of people who came to visit, especially the names of nurses, nursing assistants, and housekeepers who came and went from her room helping her.

On Thursday evening, the eleventh day after hospital discharge, I was with her when Emily, her friend and right-hand helper with the Vespers services, came for a visit. Though medicated for comfort, she was quite alert and had a good visit with Emily. The main content of their visit, however, was taken with Hannah giving Emily instructions on how to continue with Vespers as the new person in charge.

After Emily left, I stayed on for a few more hours, talking with my best friend. Eventually, Hannah fell asleep. Resting on her chest, clutched in her hand, were a small spiral notebook and a pencil. I slipped them from her hand and bid her a good rest. That evening was the last time we conversed.

I was with her all day on Friday and Friday night as she slept. Early on Saturday morning, I was awakened by a nurse who said I might want to be at Hannah's side. It was my great privilege to hold her hand, express my profound love for her, give her kisses on the forehead, weep, pray with her, and release her to the everlasting care of Almighty God to whom she had given her life as a child.

As Hannah wrote, "People watch us. They notice what we do. They hear what we say. When we become a Christian, our actions, our words, our attitudes need to reflect Christ in our lives."

Hannah, my dearest friend, beloved child of God, with your best, you made of your life an offering.

SONG 38 -

MY COURAGEOUS AND FAITHFUL MOTHER

My mother, Irma, was a mild-mannered, in-the-background kind of woman. This is not to say that she was not intelligent. She was simply satisfied with who she was and what she had. She was born in 1923. Her family, already poor, took an even harder hit when her father died suddenly from a brain aneurysm in the heart of the Great Depression. This left her mother with five children, the youngest of whom was my mother. The oldest child, Alice, married a man thirty years her senior when she was age sixteen. The second daughter, Blanche, married a man who would give her a firm financial base but keep her close to home much of the time. Mama's beloved brother, Richard, joined the military as soon as he was old enough, out of a strong sense of duty to country, and, perhaps more importantly, so he would be able to send money back home to support his mother and sisters. Beatrice, the sister next to Mama in age, who refused to answer Mama unless she called her "Sister," went to nursing school, then married. Mama, seven years old when her father died, graduated from high school then married my father, Jerry, when she was nineteen and he was twenty-three.

Mama and Daddy had a happy marriage. They grew up in low-income, rural Aurora in Eastern North Carolina, where there were few work options other than farming. Though Daddy had a brother who owned a grocery store, and another who owned a café, Daddy decided he wanted to move away for other opportunities. They moved to Baltimore where two other of his brothers and one sister lived. Then World War II came calling. Daddy, like almost all other men his age, was drafted. He was sent first to Atlantic City for basic training and was then shipped to Europe for three years. Mama remained in Baltimore, where she found a job, and lived with Daddy's brother and his wife and children. Daddy and Mama wrote letters almost every day. One day Mama did not get a letter. The next day came, no letter. And the next day. And the next day. Of course, she feared the worst. Finally, after three weeks, a letter came saying there had been a relatively minor accident and that Daddy had been blinded in one eye when struck by a wire. Both eyes had been bandaged during the period of healing, thus he had been unable to write. Soon, however, the wonderful love letters resumed.

A year after Daddy returned home from the war, and exactly one year after the atomic bomb was dropped on Hiroshima, my sister, Barbara, was born. They remained in Baltimore several more years until I was two years old, then moved back home to North Carolina. One and a half years later, my younger sister, Teresa, was born. Life was beautiful.

One day in the mid-1960s, Mama was in our yard raking leaves when, for no apparent reason, she fell. She got up but was puzzled by this. Over the following months, she fell again and again. By 1969, the situation was serious enough that she was hospitalized for a series of tests. No answers. She saw other doctors, but none could diagnose her problem. Though she had had a tremor in her hands for as long as she could remember, we never associated that condition with her falls.

Then in 1972, my father died very suddenly. Mama was forty-nine years old and was, of course, shocked and shattered. Yet she carried on bravely, at least in front of her two daughters still living at home. I wish now that I had had the courage and maturity to talk to her about her feelings, her loss, but I was too consumed with my own.

Mama never worked outside our home, so with my father's death came the challenges of supporting her children and herself, and maintaining a home. I will never really comprehend how she managed, but she did. We did not always have everything we might have wanted, but we surely had everything we needed, and often more. But the real miracle is that Mama managed to put me and Teresa both through college with the help of some scholarships and financial aid. She never complained. Instead, she was always willing to do whatever she could for all three of her daughters. After I moved away from home, more than one time she sent five or ten dollars to me in the mail. And if she did it for me, she surely did it for my sisters as well.

A funny incident happened when I was in college, living at home. I majored in music and was required to attend a certain number of concerts presented within the music department each semester. Frequently, Mama would go with me. Late one afternoon, we met for dinner at a local restaurant, planning to attend a concert afterward. It was rainy and cool, so we were both wearing raincoats. As we got about halfway through our meal, Mama said, "I hope you still have some of the money I gave you a few days ago." I answered, "No, I needed to spend it for some school things." "Well," she replied, "I'm not sure if I have enough money to pay for our food." We immediately stopped eating and, with thoughts of having to wash dishes to pay for our meals, we searched our pockets and purses. Between the two of us, we scraped together the eight or ten dollars needed to pay the bill. From then on, we checked our monies first!

From the time of Mama's first fall in the yard, she continued to fall periodically. On most occasions, she did not get hurt, but a couple of times she did fracture some ribs. Our family doctor sent her to a number of specialists, including one who tried to hypnotize Mama. Well, that was certainly not going to work for her, though she tried! During the session, which was right after lunch, she was more aware of the doctor's onion breath than anything he did or said. As the years passed, she was hospitalized in several places, including a five-week stay at the National Institutes of Health in Bethesda, Maryland, where she participated in a study. At one point, all her medications were taken away and she was so shaky she could not feed herself. I was able to be there every weekend since I was living in Richmond, Virginia at the time. It was agonizing to see her in that condition. There was never a firm diagnosis other than "familial tremor." She endured some difficult times and a few excruciating tests. But, again, she never complained. Because I had had shaky hands since I was a child, she strongly suspected that I was headed down the same road. When she went through those tests and received disappointing results, she would invariably say, "Well, if this doesn't help me, maybe it will help you or someone else." It turns out that both I and my younger sister inherited the same disease, and what Mama endured did, indeed, help advance the understanding of the disease. How often Teresa and I have wished she could have benefitted more.

In the mid-1980s, Mama's oldest sister, Alice, and the sister she called "Sister" were both diagnosed with cancer, but entirely different kinds. Mama spent a good bit of time with Aunt Alice, helping her two daughters care for her and taking advantage of what little time Aunt Alice had left to live. She died a difficult death, which took a toll on Mama. "Sister" lived longer. Since she had a husband and a larger family, including a daughter who was a nurse, and lived a little farther away, Mama did not go there as frequently, but they kept in close contact. They had a special bond from childhood.

"Sister" died on Easter Sunday, which her entire family celebrated as a special gift of grace from God. The funeral was mid-week. I had already planned vacation for that week, so after the funeral, Mama and I went to the beach for a few days. She had not been feeling well for several months, but when I saw her in shorts at the beach, I knew something was very wrong. She was thinner than I had ever seen her. My sisters and I had known she was losing weight, but this was more than we had observed.

Mama was soon hospitalized. Over a five-week period, many tests and an exploratory surgery were done. Finally, when we learned the diagnosis, we also learned that the survival rate for the particular kind of cancer she had was only about five percent. But Mama bravely moved forward.

She was discharged home and began out-patient chemotherapy, then had six weeks of radiation, and then more chemo. While I was terrified, angry, and extremely sad at the prospect of losing my sweet, gentle mother and priceless friend, she outwardly showed more courage than sadness.

When I say courage, I do not mean Mama talked about being courageous. No, she did not talk about courage or bravery or her fight for life, just as she did not talk extensively about her faith. But both were always present. She *lived* them, both her courage and her faith. Courage and faith were the basis of her life. They sustained her daily and provided a solid foundation when she was most in need. They brought her joy in the form of family, friends, and opportunities for serving God. They gave purpose to her life. Faith and courage anchored her.

During the seven months from the diagnosis until her death, Mama was in and out of the hospital for ninety days. Many of those days were extremely hard. But in the end, she died with my sister, Teresa, at her side. Mama was no longer in pain and was at peace. A peace only a faithful, courageous woman can know.

Thank you, Mama, for your selfless love and for the life lessons you demonstrated in your living and in your dying, in your courage and in your faith. We are the family and the individuals we are, and the world is a better place, because of you.

SONG 39 –

A SONG FOR ALL THE PEOPLE

The stories you have read are as true as my mind and heart remember them. In more instances than not, I have been able to share the "songs" and confirm facts with family members of those whose stories I tell. I offer my deepest gratitude to all individuals and families who have granted enthusiastic and generous permission to include the story of someone they have loved and still cherish in their hearts and minds.

In some cases, there is no family still living. I have taken this as permission to use real names. And in a few instances, I have been unable to locate family members. Therefore, names have been changed or omitted altogether in some stories. I sincerely hope that any family member who might recognize a story I have told will know that it has come from deep in my heart, and will share in my warm remembrances.

There is one thing I feel compelled to share that I would not have thought to write before 2020. This book has been written, for the most part, in the spring and summer of 2020, in the middle of the unprecedented worldwide coronavirus pandemic, and amid the uprising of those who have been the unfortunate heirs of centuries of racism. The stories I have told have been personal to me. The stories of hundreds of thousands, even millions world-wide, who have died of COVID-19 cannot be personal in the same way. Since I am a white American, I cannot know the pain systemically inflicted on people of color or other ethnic origin. Yet all of us are human, equally loved by God. Each person who has died has had a story. Each person who struggles to be treated with dignity and full humanity has a story. Each person who has died has been a song in someone's night. Each person who has lost one person, or two people, or several people, grieves deeply. Each person who is desperate for change in the hearts of humankind is longing. Some lives have been irreparably changed. For others, little or no change seems yet in sight. Not everyone's story has an uplifting ending. However, some survivors find a way through their grief and pain to see *the life that is real even in the midst of death and suffering.* May God bless them all. May God bless us all.

Thank you, God, my Song in the night, for giving us life even in the midst of death.

HARK! I HEAR THE HARPS ETERNAL

Hark! I hear the harps eternal,

Ringing on the farther shore.

As I near those swollen waters,

With their deep and solemn roar.

Hallelujah, hallelujah, hallelujah, praise the Lamb!

Hallelujah, hallelujah, Glory to the great I AM!

Souls have cross'd before me, saintly,

To that land of perfect rest;

And I hear them singing faintly,

In the mansions of the blest.

Hallelujah, hallelujah, hallelujah, praise the Lamb!

Hallelujah, hallelujah, Glory to the great I AM!

First published in the 1854 edition of *Southern Harmony*
Attributed to F.R. Warren
(Public Domain)